Health Matters

Health Awareness for College Students

TETSURO FUJII   ADAM MURRAY

KINSEIDO

Kinseido Publishing Co., Ltd.
3-21 Kanda Jimbo-cho, Chiyoda-ku,
Tokyo 101-0051, Japan

Copyright © 2009 by Tetsuro Fujii
       Adam Murray

All rights reserved. No part of this publication
may be reproduced, stored in a retrieval system,
or transmitted, in any form or by any means,
electronic, mechanical, photocopying, recording
or otherwise, without the prior permission of
the publisher.

Cover Design: Hull corporation
Text Design: IOK Co., Ltd.
Illustrations: Jun Koito

The Intentions Behind *Health Matters*

Words form the basis of all communication. However, the words that come out of our mouths can inadvertently cause miscommunication and misunderstandings. Even the most innocuous question like "How long have you been here?" can be interpreted in a variety of ways. "Here" can refer to this room, this class, this school, this country, etc. depending on the neighboring words. As Firth so aptly put it, "You shall know a word by the company it keeps!" *

We must keep reminding ourselves that language is an imperfect medium of communication and thus, it entails the constant negotiation of meaning. Learning a foreign language (using an inter-language) is the best reminder of this crucial fact. It puts us in the listener's shoes and makes us appreciate different perspectives and value systems; at the same time, we reconsider our own views. Eventually, we see that recognition and even culture are not absolute but relative.

This course book makes the students communicate in English, however imperfect it might be, and helps to develop meta-cognitive skills — i.e. they can have insight into how they can best convey their intended message and why the listener did not interpret words in the anticipated way.

Since they are using a foreign language, they are put in a situation where nothing can be taken for granted. Naturally, they make mistakes and struggle through the communication process. Let them know beforehand that mistakes are good. Mistakes are constructive if the students learn from them and do not run away from them. In this way, students become more comfortable with the learning process of miscommunication and improvement through using the language.

In selecting the content topics, we chose themes that are universal as well as timeless because much of the content taught in college (especially in science classes) will be either outdated or forgotten after graduation. Likewise some global issues are too general and difficult for students to relate to. Health-related topics, on the other hand, are palpable, relatable and are of interest to students in general classes as well as people in health-care related fields. Furthermore, this textbook avoids the presentation of medical jargon, and instead uses common vocabulary that is understandable to lay people or patients.

In addition to raising health awareness, this book includes activities to develop language and critical thinking skills. Of course, these skills are not specific to health-care and can be applied to other contexts. Learners will take a critical look at the issues presented and discuss them in a logical manner, and hopefully learn to distinguish facts from misinformation in this information-abundant society.

In conclusion, we the authors hope that the variety of themes presented in this book will provide students with opportunities to not only learn new information but also to become more aware of their own health and start a life-long process of developing a healthy lifestyle while building their communication and thinking skills.

Acknowledgements

We would like to thank Paul Rowan for providing insightful input on the listening sections and the model dialogues. We would also like to thank Michael Pronko for jazzing up the model dialogues with colorful expressions.

Adam MURRAY and Tetsuro FUJII

---

*Palmer (1968) (ed.): "A Synopsis of Linguistic Theory, 1930-55," Selected Papers of J.R. Firth 1952-59, Longman, p. 179.

How to Use *Health Matters*

Unit Title has been designed to elicit the students' background knowledge and to help develop schema. Use this as a prompt for warm-up questions.

MATCHING encourages students to first skim through the headwords and then to peruse the definitions and synonyms. Choosing the correct definition naturally leads students to think about an item's part of speech — an essential skill for effective use of an English-English dictionary. After finishing the exercise, the students close their books and listen to the teacher say the definitions and synonyms. They then guess which headword the teacher is talking about.

GAP-FILL EXERCISE allows students to use words in context. After completing this exercise, the students close their books and listen to the teacher read aloud one of the sentences — e.g. "Can you be more BLANK?" They guess which word best fills the blank.

VOCABULARY ANALOGIES require students to think more deeply about the meanings and the relationships of several words. This aims to increase vocabulary retention and develop the use of logical and analytical skills. To get the maximum benefit from this exercise, always discuss the reasons why X is the correct answer, as in the following example:

> **Socks** are to **feet** as **gloves** are to _____.
> A. hand   B. foot   C. hands

The correct answer is C. Why? It's because socks are worn on one's feet and gloves are worn on one's hands. "Feet" is a plural noun so **A** is incorrect because "hand" is a singular noun.
Another format is like this: **A** is to same to **B** as **C** is to **D**
Please note that **A** is never related to **D**.

BEFORE YOU LISTEN activates students' general background knowledge of the topic and facilitates purposeful listening. Students will listen to understand how the talk is organized and try to get the gist, just as they would by skimming a text. Students may be asked to close their books and they would listen to the teacher say the three questions. They should be ready to take notes.

LISTEN section is first used as a listening task, but if the students have difficulty answering some of the questions in **BEFORE YOU LISTEN** and **CHECK YOUR COMPREHENSION**, let them read the passage or scan it as quickly as possible and find the answers to those difficult question items.

CHECK YOUR COMPREHENSION tests understanding of overall concepts, as well as specific details of the passage. Their books may remain closed, and students will listen to the teacher read aloud the five questions one by one. The students will discuss each of them with each other in order to find the answers.

QUESTIONS AND ANSWERS requires students to form pairs. They will memorize a few questions to ask each other in order to fill the information gaps. Alternatively, the entire class can be divided into two groups. Students walk around the classroom and ask one question to a person in the other group, starting and ending the conversation as follows: Hi! Izumi, How are you? May I ask a question? . . . Thank you. Bye. See you later.

MODEL DIALOGUE – JIGSAW LISTENING is a pair-work activity that requires students to listen to the model recording (which is also included on the Student CD) and complete the dialogue. After listening to the recording two or three times, partners can help each other to say the dialogue properly.

ACT OUT THE DIALOGUE is a challenging task of reproduction. Students have to imagine themselves in the situation. Make it as real as possible. They can use their own names to make it even more realistic. Although they are allowed to look down and read the text one line at a time, they have to look up and make eye contact with their partner like a normal exchange. It should be naturally supplemented with gestures, physical expressions, and augmented with intonations and tone of voice, etc. Since the dialogues are included on the Student CD, the students can practice even when they do not have a conversation partner. A teacher may ask students to demonstrate the dialogue in front of the class.

FACT DICTATION can be completed by listening to the recording two or three times as group work or pair work. When giving the answers, a teacher may have the students close their books and give just the first few words of each sentence as a clue and let the students finish it.

IN YOUR OWN WORDS provides a creative outlet. Students expands upon what is written in the text. Students may work in a group and discuss the items and come up with a group consensus or simply appreciate the differences of opinions as well as be fascinated by the similarities. If the discussion seems to be going well, this section can be developed into an essay-writing or presentation project.

CRITICAL THINKING includes a few types of fallacies. The seemingly benign statements presented are, in fact, all wrong. There are no sound reasons to establish causal relationships within the statements. Teacher will ask students to explain why the given statement is wrong. Moreover, students may be asked to create another fallacious statement of the same kind. See the subheading of this section for the fallacy type.

Student CD includes **ASSIGNMENT DICTATION**: four statements and one personal question for each unit. The statements and the question are read twice. The first time is at natural speed for listening practice and the second time is at a reduced speed for listen & repeat practice. Students write down every word in the four sentences and write a personalized answer to the given question so that they cannot copy their classmates' assignments.

Student CD also includes **MODEL DIALOGUE** for a student to practice conversation without a conversation partner. The audio for speaker A is recorded in one channel and the audio for speaker B is recorded in the other channel. For example, if a student wants to practice the lines for speaker B, they listen to only the recording of speaker A by using only one earphone and responding at the appropriate times. Of course, by listening with the other earphone, the lines for speaker A can also be practiced.

CONTENTS

Unit	Title	Page
1	Why English? — The Basis for Academic Inquiry	7
2	Sleep — Sweet Dreams	13
3	Allergies — Got an Itch to Scratch?	19
4	Stress Management — Don't Let it Get to You!	25
5	Skin — Beauty is Only Skin Deep	31
6	Sports Injuries — RICE is Nice	37
	Review Unit 1-6: TOEHM (Test of English for Health Matters)	43
7	Personality — You Need to Chill Out!	49
8	Nutrition — Nutritious is Delicious	55
9	Aromatherapy — What's that Smell?	61
10	Aging — Forever Young	67
11	Acupuncture — On Pins and Needles	73
12	Three Major Causes of Death — Are You Insured?	79
	Review Unit 7-12: TOEHM (Test of English for Health Matters)	85
	Student B pages	91
	Glossary	116
	Task Sheets	121

Unit 1

Why English? The Basis for Academic Inquiry

MATCHING

Match the words (1-8) with the correct definitions (a-h).
1. ___ duty
2. ___ lingua franca
3. ___ realize
4. ___ scholar
5. ___ billion
6. ___ remedy
7. ___ curiosity
8. ___ specific

a. the number 1,000,000,000
b. the desire to know about something
c. something that you have to do because it is morally or legally right
d. a language used between people whose main languages are different
e. to know and understand something, or suddenly begin to understand it
f. a medicine to cure an illness or pain that is not very serious
g. an intelligent and well-educated person
h. detailed and exact

GAP-FILL EXERCISE

Complete the sentences with the words from MATCHING.
1. "Art is the lie that enables us to _____ the truth."
   ——*Pablo Picasso, painter*
2. The police have a _____ to protect the public.
3. "Our sun is one of 100 _____ stars in our galaxy."
   ——*Wernher von Braun, scientist*
4. Can you be more _____ ?
5. In the past, French was the _____ of diplomacy.
6. _____ killed the cat.
7. "To do nothing is also a good _____ ." ——*Hippocrates, physician*

7

VOCABULARY ANALOGIES

Analogies show how words are related. For example, LISTEN is to SOUND as SEE is to SIGHT.

1. **Student** is to **college** as **scholar** is to _____.
   a. beliefs   **b.** knowledge   **c.** academia
2. **Thousand** is to **three** as **billion** is to _____.
   a. nine   **b.** six   **c.** ten
3. **Universal** is to **universe** as **curious** is to _____.
   a. cure   **b.** curiosity   **c.** curable
4. **Require** is to **need** as **duty** is to _____.
   a. responsibility **b.** imagination **c.** information
5. **Difficult** is to **easy** as **common** is to _____.
   a. perfect   **b.** rare   **c.** even
6. **Access** is to **reach** as **specific** is to _____.
   a. particular   **b.** global   **c.** general
7. **Caught** is to **trapped** as **realize** is to _____.
   a. communicate **b.** shortage   **c.** notice

BEFORE YOU LISTEN

Listen for answers to the following questions.
1. Who studies English? Where do they learn English?
2. Why is studying English necessary?
3. What is the role of English?

LISTEN

Close the textbook and take notes about the key information.

   Is English a required subject at your university? Almost all universities, not only in this country but also in other countries require all students to study English and to communicate in English, but why? It's because more than 90 percent of new information in the world is first reported *(5)* in English through research papers, presentations, journal articles and on the Internet. Let's imagine that Korean scientists discovered a specific medicine for the common cold virus. They would report it in English so that many scientists in other countries could also test their findings. *(10)* If not, this medical knowledge would be unknown to 3.53

Unit 1
Why English? The Basis for Academic Inquiry

billion other people around the world and the remedy would never become universal.

    If a family member or friend got a particularly rare disease, using English would increase the chances of finding the cure because somewhere in the world there are other people with the same disease. Sir Francis Bacon said "knowledge is power," but if the *(15)* information leading to this knowledge is written only in Hangul, it has to be translated into English in order for people in the global village to learn about it. English is the key to access this information. Without English, it would be extremely difficult, if not impossible, to learn about the most advanced sciences, medicines, and technologies of the world. Without English, you face a shortage of information and may be trapped *(20)* in the world of the unknown without even realizing it! That is not the life of college students or scholars in academia. You have a great curiosity to ask questions nobody has ever asked, find the answers to these questions, and tell your findings to people around the world. This is your duty and responsibility, and all of this is done in English as a part of academic conversation. That's why English reading and writing are required *(25)* subjects in universities all over the world. Although English may not be the perfect tool of communication, it is used as a lingua franca, the universal language in our global community.

CHECK YOUR COMPREHENSION

1. Answer the following questions.
   1. Where is new information first presented?
   2. What percentage of new information is presented in English?
   3. Why do findings need to be reported in English?
   4. What did Sir Francis Bacon say about knowledge?
   5. What does the term "lingua franca" mean?

2. Correct the following statements.
   1. Ninety percent of all information in the world is reported in English.
   2. English decreases the chances of finding cures for rare diseases.
   3. Hangul is the necessary tool to access new information.
   4. You can learn about advanced sciences without using English.
   5. English is not a required subject at most universities around the world.

QUESTIONS AND ANSWERS — People Who Use English

Student A (Student B, see page 92)

a. Memorize and ask these questions to Student B and complete your chart.
1. What is (Alfred)'s first language?
2. What is (Alfred)'s occupation?
3. Where does (Alfred) work?
4. What English journal does (Alfred) read?

Name	First Language	Occupation	Department/ Workplace	Name of Journal
Alfred		nurse		*Nature*
Benjamin	Korean		surgery	
Charlie		dentist		*New England Journal of Medicine*
David	Thai		gynecology	
Edward		dietitian		*Lancet*
Frank	Spanish		psychiatry	

b. Answer the following questions.
1. Who should you go to if you are pregnant?
2. Who would you go to if your child got sick?
3. What language do you use when reading websites?

Unit 1
Why English? The Basis for Academic Inquiry

MODEL DIALOGUE — JIGSAW LISTENING

Student A (Student B, see page 93)

Listen, repeat and fill in the blanks.

A: Hi, Judy, how's your _____ _____ going?

B: Hi, Ed, I'm learning so much. I feel like a kid again!

A: That's great to _____ like that. I'm just the _____. My classes are _____ boring, and nothing _____ to my major.

B: So, that's why it's good to take other classes, isn't it? You need to learn things outside your specialty. That makes you more well-rounded.

A: I'm really only _____ in my _____.

B: Oh, come on! Don't tell me you don't care about the big questions in life, who we are, where we are going, or how the world works?

A: My major is medicine, so I'll _____ be studying that the _____ of my life. Why should I _____ time with all those _____ things?

B: Of course, you are majoring in medicine, yet you study English, too. What about that?

A: I study English because I _____ to. It's _____. I wouldn't _____ otherwise. How about yourself?

B: I'm learning a foreign language because it shows me different ways of thinking. It opens my mind up and gets my brain working in new ways.

A: Uh, I've never _____ about it _____ that. I only _____ Japanese to think.

B: Then your ability to think is limited to just one way. That's too boring, don't you think?

ACT OUT THE DIALOGUE

Work with your partner.
1. Silently and quickly read and remember one line at a time.
2. Look up at your partner and speak while keeping eye contact.
3. Change roles and practice again by replacing some parts with your own words.

11

FACT DICTATION

Here are some interesting facts. Listen and fill in the blanks.

1. In the world of scholarship, you _____ _____ _____ _____ write a thesis in English.

2. It will be _____ evaluated _____ printed _____ _____ in English.

3. It's _____ _____ _____ _____ and common knowledge in many _____ fields.

4. However, freshmen and sophomores _____ _____ do not _____ this fact.

5. After _____ _____ and seniors, they _____ that they must read and write English for their _____ .

6. Subsequently, they _____ the _____ of their vocabulary and grammatical knowledge.

7. They _____ _____ _____ of English competence, and English _____ _____ _____ _____ academic communication.

IN YOUR OWN WORDS

a. List three reasons why you learn English.
 •   •   •

b. Name three effective ways to learn English.
 •   •   •

CRITICAL THINKING — An argument against the person

Explain what is wrong with the following statement:
 An English teacher said, "Clinicians need English to learn new things." He is not a doctor and never practiced nor studied medicine. Thus, his comment is wrong.

Unit 2

Sleep — Sweet Dreams

MATCHING

Match the words (1-10) with the correct definitions (a-j).

1. ___ brag
2. ___ fatigue
3. ___ colleague
4. ___ accomplish
5. ___ chronic
6. ___ deprivation
7. ___ average
8. ___ drowsy
9. ___ sacrifice
10. ___ achievement

a. to complete something successfully
b. continuing for a long time
c. to speak arrogantly
d. dull and sleepy
e. to give up or surrender something
f. typical of most people or things
g. a fellow worker; an associate
h. extreme mental or physical exhaustion
i. shortage of something
j. something successful that is achieved after a lot of effort

GAP-FILL EXERCISE

Complete the sentences with the words from MATCHING.

1. The unlucky child has _____ asthma.
2. "It's not _____ ing if you can back it up." ——*Muhammad Ali, boxer*
3. Don't _____ your health for your job.
4. Winning an Olympic medal is a great _____.
5. _____ is a lack of energy and motivation.
6. "I'm not the smartest fellow in the world, but I can sure pick smart _____ s." ——*Franklin D. Roosevelt, U.S. President*
7. Sleep _____ and sleep disorders are quite common.

13

VOCABULARY ANALOGIES

Analogies show how words are related. For example, LISTEN is to SOUND as SEE is to SIGHT.

1. **Sleepiness** is to **nap** as **fatigue** is to _____.
   a. cheating **b.** rest **c.** survival
2. **Gathering** is to **collect** as **sacrificing** is to _____.
   a. make up **b.** stock up **c.** give up
3. **Energy** is to **shortage** as **sleep** is to _____.
   a. deprivation **b.** necessary **c.** torture
4. **Focus** is to **concentration** as **results** is to _____.
   a. seriousness **b.** unfortunate **c.** consequences
5. **Refreshed** is to **tired** as **awake** is to _____.
   a. energetic **b.** drowsy **c.** relaxed
6. **Achieve** is to **achievement** as **accomplish** is to _____.
   a. accomplishment **b.** completion **c.** success
7. **Short-term** is to **temporary** as **long-term** is to _____.
   a. chronic **b.** acute **c.** sudden

BEFORE YOU LISTEN

Listen for answers to the following questions.
1. What is the main topic of this talk?
2. What does sleep deprivation mean?
3. What problems are caused by a lack of sleep?

LISTEN

Close the textbook and take notes about the key information.

From tiny flies to huge elephants, all animals sleep. Sleeping is essential for our survival. It's just as important as eating. For the average adult to lead a healthy life, doctors recommend (5) sleeping seven to eight hours. However, some people brag about sacrificing sleep for their work. They say something like "I was up all night finishing my work," "I burnt the midnight oil for the (10) exam," and "I only took a short nap in my office." When you hear these things from your boss or colleagues, realize that they are not really talking about how hard they work. They are actually commenting on their unhealthy lifestyles. Just because people around you work like that, it doesn't mean you have to do the same. You are not expected *(15)* to lose sleep over your work.

Sleep deprivation, a lack of sleep, has serious consequences. It causes people to feel drowsy, lose concentration, make mistakes and even causes accidents. You need a good night's sleep every day. Don't think that you can cheat sleep. You cannot make up for a lack of sleep on weekdays by sleeping more on weekends. You need to keep the *(20)* same sleep schedule seven days a week. If you don't, you may be in a chronic state of jet lag. You are awake, but you don't feel fully awake. You always feel sleepy, and day-by-day, you build up fatigue. However, oddly enough, some people do not feel tired at all especially after finishing a big project. This is because they get a sense of achievement from the work done and they forget their tiredness. Surely, a sense of accomplishment *(25)* gets you excited, but it does not refresh your body or mind. Only getting enough sleep truly relaxes your brain, and at the same time, it allows the brain to stock up on energy and review all the information gathered while awake. So, study before going to bed, sleep tight and have sweet dreams.

CHECK YOUR COMPREHENSION

a. Answer the following questions.
1. To be healthy, how many hours should people sleep?
2. What do some unhealthy people say about sacrificing sleep?
3. What does sleep deprivation cause?
4. What can happen if you do not keep the same sleep schedule?
5. How can people truly relax their brain?

b. Correct the following statements.
1. You don't need to maintain the same sleeping schedule every day.
2. Some people brag about how much they sleep.
3. Sleep deprivation is a surplus of sleep.
4. A sense of accomplishment refreshes your body.
5. While sleeping, the brain gathers new energy.

QUESTIONS AND ANSWERS — Sleeping Habits

Student A (Student B, see page 94)

a. Memorize and ask these questions to Student B and complete your chart.
   1. Is (Alfred) ever late for class?
   2. What time does (Alfred) usually go to sleep?
   3. What does (Alfred) do before going to bed?
   4. How long does (Alfred) sleep every day?

Name	Late for Class	Bed Time	Before Bed	Sleeping Hours
Alfred		1 a.m.		five hours
Benjamin	often		watches TV	
Charlie		11 o'clock		six hours
David	never		reads	
You				
Partner				

b. Answer the following questions.
   1. Who gets up earliest?
   2. Who sleeps the longest?
   3. Who has the healthiest sleeping habits?

Unit 2
Sleep — Sweet Dreams

MODEL DIALOGUE — JIGSAW LISTENING

Student A (Student B, see page 95)

Listen, repeat and fill in the blanks.

A: Hi, John, _____ _____ _____ _____?

B: Oh, hi, Sara, I'm a little sleepy today. I felt drowsy all day yesterday.

A: What _____ to be the _____?

B: I haven't gotten much sleep lately. I think I might have insomnia.

A: What time _____ you _____ go to _____?

B: About 12 o'clock, after watching TV and drinking beer.

A: I've _____ TV and _____ just make insomnia _____.

B: Maybe. It seems that way these days. How about you? What do you usually do before going to bed?

A: I usually do some _____ and drink a _____ of _____ milk.

B: Does that work?

A: Almost _____, yes.

B: So, you never have trouble falling asleep?

A: Not _____. I've never used sleeping _____, either. Just a good _____ and some _____.

B: I never take pills, either, but I definitely need a better sleep cycle.

ACT OUT THE DIALOGUE

Work with a partner.

1. Silently and quickly read and remember one line at a time.
2. Look up at your partner and speak while keeping eye contact.
3. Change roles and practice again by replacing some parts with information about yourself.

FACT DICTATION

Here are some interesting facts and tips about sleep. Listen and fill in the blanks.

1. After you get sunlight, _____ _____ _____ 14 to 16 hours _____ your body _____ prepare to sleep.

2. The best bed _____ is 33 degrees Celsius plus or minus 1 degree; the best _____, 50% _____ or _____ 5%.

3. For a good night's sleep, _____ _____ _____ _____ a 20-minute-nap before 3 p.m.

4. To sleep well, _____ your body _____ by waking up the _____ _____ every day.

5. Don't _____ _____ on weekends because it will _____ up your sleep schedule.

6. Finish your meal _____ _____ three hours before bedtime. _____ _____ at least two hours before bedtime.

7. Don't _____ _____ _____ before going to bed: Avoid fast tempo music, _____ and even _____ food.

IN YOUR OWN WORDS

a. List three common problems associated with insomnia.
 ·   ·   ·

b. Name three effective ways to fall asleep.
 ·   ·   ·

CRITICAL THINKING — Hasty generalization

Explain what is wrong with the following statement:
  Napoleon is said to have slept only three hours a day. All of us can do with as few as three hours of sleep every day.

Unit 3

Allergies — Got an Itch to Scratch?

MATCHING

Match the words (1-8) with the correct definitions (a-h).

1. ___ exposure
2. ___ immune
3. ___ symptom
4. ___ particular
5. ___ occur
6. ___ disorder
7. ___ intake
8. ___ estimate

a. a mental or physical illness which prevents part of your body from working properly
b. to judge the value, size, speed, cost, etc., of something without calculating exactly
c. the situation where you have no protection from something harmful, dangerous or unpleasant
d. protected from and resistant to a certain disease
e. the amount of food, drink, etc. that you take into your body
f. to happen
g. specific, certain or distinct; not general
h. a sign that shows there is something wrong with your body or mind

GAP-FILL EXERCISE

Complete the sentences with the words from MATCHING.

1. Try to reduce your _____ of fat.
2. Cancer is a major concern from asbestos _____.
3. He has a rare blood _____.
4. This _____ part of the country is very beautiful.
5. They _____ that the cherry tree is over 700 years old.
6. Some people are _____ to the virus.
7. "The first _____ of love in a man is shyness." ——*Victor Hugo, poet*
8. Hundreds of earthquakes _____ everyday around the world.

VOCABULARY ANALOGIES

Analogies show how words are related. For example, LISTEN is to SOUND as SEE is to SIGHT.

1. **Controlled** is to **uncontrolled** as **runny** is to _____.
   a. fits   **b.** sneezing   **c.** stuffy
2. **React** is to **overreact** as **sensitive** is to _____.
   a. oversimplify   **b.** oversensitive   **c.** overact
3. **Foreign** is to **unfamiliar** as **materials** is to _____.
   a. substances   **b.** diseases   **c.** allergies
4. **Cedar** is to **tree** as **pollen** is to _____.
   a. allergen   **b.** symptom   **c.** sufferer
5. **Calculate** is to **estimate** as **problem** is to _____.
   a. cities   **b.** pollution   **c.** challenge
6. **Mountain** is to **mountainous** as **symptom** is to _____.
   a. illness   **b.** symptomatic   **c.** treatments
7. **Eyes** is to **itchy** as **nose** is to _____.
   a. sneezing   **b.** hay fever   **c.** intake

BEFORE YOU LISTEN

Listen for answers to the following questions.
1. What happens when you have an allergy?
2. What is a common allergy in Japan?
3. What can you do to prevent allergies?

LISTEN

Close the textbook and take notes about the key information.

Do you have fits of sneezing, a runny or stuffy nose? If you do, you may have a common cold. However, if you have itchy eyes and cannot stop rubbing them when you are outside, or some part of your skin gets red and painful, what you have may not be a common cold but an allergy. Do you know how an allergic reaction occurs?

Our body has an immune system that protects our body against diseases. It finds *(5)* and fights foreign substances in our body. However, it sometimes becomes oversensitive and overreacts to particular substances like pollen. Pollen is an allergen that causes a great number of allergies. In particular, allergies to cedar tree pollen are a serious public health challenge in Japan. The government estimates there are between ten and 15 million sufferers. Currently, available therapies focus on symptom relief, yet there are still a lot *(10)* of people with uncontrolled symptoms. That is because symptomatic treatments do not treat the immune system disorder.

Unit 3

Allergies — Got an Itch to Scratch?

Cedar allergies are rare in Okinawa and Hokkaido, where cedar trees are scarce or nonexistent. In general, it is also true that people living in mountainous areas covered with cedars suffer a lot less from pollen allergies than people living in cities. What is the likely cause of this? Experts point their fingers at air pollution. Laboratory experiments have shown that mixing allergens with diesel exhaust increase the chances of allergic reactions. In fact, in areas where there are many automobiles, there are more people with hay fever. *(15) (20) (25)*

As a prevention, doctors recommend wearing a mask to reduce the amount of pollen intake through your nose by 80%, wearing glasses to reduce exposure to the eyes by 50% and cleaning the inside of your nose with saline, salty water. *(30)*

CHECK YOUR COMPREHENSION

a. Answer the following questions.
1. What is the purpose of the immune system?
2. How many people suffer from allergies in Japan?
3. What do current therapies focus on?
4. How can you reduce pollen intake?
5. What is saline?

b. Correct the following statements.
1. Symptomatic treatments treat immune system disorders.
2. Many people in Hokkaido have cedar allergies.
3. Pollution causes allergic reactions.
4. A mask can increase pollen intake by 80%.
5. Doctors recommend cleaning the outside of your nose with saline.

21

QUESTIONS AND ANSWERS — Allergies

Student A (Student B, see page 96)

a. Memorize and ask these questions to Student B and complete your chart.
 1. What seems to be (Edward)'s problem?
 2. What can be a cause of allergy to (Edward)?
 3. What does (Edward) do to prevent the allergy?
 4. What (medicine) does (Edward) take to cure the symptom?

Name	Problem / Symptom	Causes of the Allergy	Ways to Prevent	Medicine
Edward		cedar trees		eye drops
Frank	fits of sneezing		wearing a mask	
George		crab meat or shrimp		ointment
Harry	nausea		reading food labels and checking ingredients	
You				
Partner				

b. Answer the following questions.
 1. Whose allergy seems to be the most severe? Why?
 2. What are other ways to cure allergies?
 3. Whose allergy seems to be the most curable? Why?

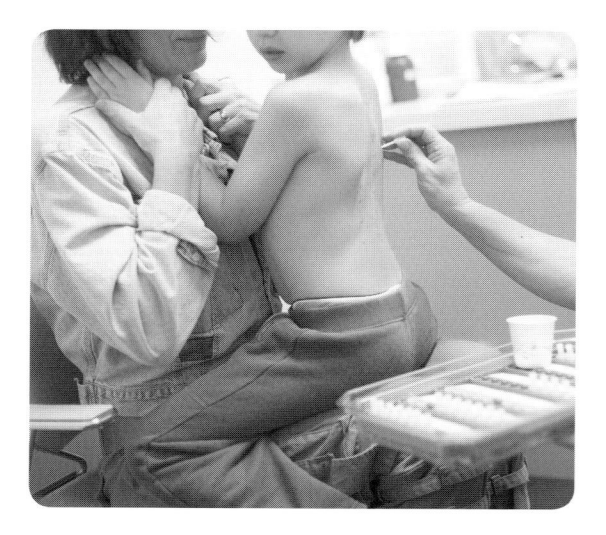

Unit 3
Allergies — Got an Itch to Scratch?

MODEL DIALOGUE — JIGSAW LISTENING

Student A (Student B, see page 97)

Listen, repeat and fill in the blanks.

A: Hello, Mr. Takeda. What _____ to _____ the _____ today?

B: Hello, doctor. I have a stuffy nose, no matter how much I blow my nose.

A: I can _____ your nose is _____ up, with a bit of a _____ _____ your voice, too. Does your throat _____ _____?

B: Yes, and my eyes are scratchy, too. Really, it itches everywhere.

A: What _____ is your _____? Is it yellow or _____ like water?

B: Like water. My eyes are watering all the time, too.

A: When did all this _____? Any _____ time?

B: It started right after I moved to a new apartment.

A: Did you _____ anything _____ in the new _____?

B. It's a little old and very dusty, but there's nothing unusual about it.

A: Does this _____ all the time, _____ every year _____ the spring or …?

B: No, it has never happened to me before.

A: Well, _____. You might have _____ _____ to house _____.

B: What does that mean? Is there anything I can do about it? Do I have to move again?

ACT OUT THE DIALOGUE

Work with your partner.
1. Silently and quickly read and remember one line at a time.
2. Look up at your partner and speak while keeping eye contact.
3. Change roles and practice again by replacing some parts with your own words.

FACT DICTATION

Here are some interesting facts. Listen and fill in the blanks.

1. It's really hard to _____ _____ _____ cold germs or pollens, especially _____ .
2. Make sure you _____ _____ your nose _____ _____ with your mouth.
3. The nose _____ _____ _____ to about 30 degrees and _____ it to about 90%.
4. It also cleans _____ and viruses with cilia, _____ hairs _____ _____ of your nose.
5. Cilia, _____ _____ _____ _____ the mucus membrane, slowly _____ bacteria and viruses _____ the food pipe to the stomach.
6. Bacteria and _____ are killed _____ _____ stomach.
7. This _____ _____ from 40 minutes to _____ hour.

IN YOUR OWN WORDS

a. List three common causes of allergies.
-
-
-

b. Name three effective ways to treat allergies.
-
-
-

CRITICAL THINKING — Confusing sequence with consequence

Explain what is wrong with the following statement:

After I got to this outdoor cypress hot spring, I began to sneezing continuously. Thus, the cause of my allergy to cypresses is this bathtub.

Unit 4

Stress Management— Don't Let it Get to You!

MATCHING

Match the words (1-10) with the correct definitions (a-j).

1. ___ diaphragm
2. ___ respond
3. ___ exhale
4. ___ major
5. ___ shallowly
6. ___ backwards
7. ___ unusual
8. ___ increase
9. ___ wander
10. ___ breath

a. in a reverse manner or order
b. the air that you send out of your lungs when you breathe
c. the muscle between your lungs and your stomach, used for breathing
d. to breathe air, smoke, and so on out of your mouth
e. becoming bigger in amount, number, or degree
f. important, big, serious, significant
g. to do something as a reaction to something that has been said or done
h. superficially, not deeply
i. different from what is usual or normal
j. to walk slowly across or around an area, without a purpose

GAP-FILL EXERCISE

Complete the sentences with the words from MATCHING.

1. The doctor told me to count _____ from ten to one.
2. The _____ is the main muscle of inspiration.
3. "If you want to _____ your success rate, double your failure rate."
   ——*Tom Watson, golfer*
4. Crime is a _____ problem in that city.
5. Why didn't you _____ to my emails?
6. Planting a tree too _____ or too deeply is a common failure in transplanting.
7. I like to _____ around shopping malls.

VOCABULARY ANALOGIES

Analogies show how words are related. For example, LISTEN is to SOUND as SEE is to SIGHT.

1. **Action** is to **reaction** as **question** is to _____.
   a. response   **b.** problem   **c.** trouble
2. **Outstanding** is to **outstand** as **breathing** is to _____.
   a. breath   **b.** breathe   **c.** breathed
3. **Stress** is to **stressor** as **tense** is to _____.
   a. feel   **b.** causes   **c.** tension
4. **Effective** is to **ineffective** as **positive** is to _____.
   a. negative   **b.** events   **c.** noses
5. **Usual** is to **unusual** as **deep** is to _____.
   a. empty   **b.** natural   **c.** shallow
6. **A little** is to **slightly** as **exhale** is to _____.
   a. inhale   **b.** breath   **c.** breathe out
7. **Food** is to **stomach** as **air** is to _____.
   a. abdominal   **b.** lungs   **c.** pause

BEFORE YOU LISTEN

Listen for answers to the following questions.
1. What is stress?
2. What causes stress?
3. What is a technique that can be used to manage stress?

LISTEN

Close the textbook and take notes about the key information.

Are you under stress right now? Do you feel stress in your daily life? Although you may not notice stress, stress is always there.

What is stress? Scientifically speaking, it is simply the body's response to any event. This may result in faster breathing, faster heart rate and increased blood pressure. Muscles can become tense. *(5)*

Something that creates stress is called a stressor. In general, any event in our life can be a stressor. Somebody's death, divorce, separation from partners, major injuries or illnesses and being fired at work are all examples of negative events that are great stressors. Not only that, even some positive events like marriage, pregnancy and outstanding personal achievement can be stressors, too. Stress in itself is not so *(10)* dangerous, but rather the danger is in how you respond to stressful situations, be they positive or negative. That's the reason we need to learn effective ways to cope with stress.

Unit 4

Stress Management — Don't Let it Get to You!

One quick way to release stress is proper breathing. For some reason, people nowadays breathe very shallowly and it's not at all unusual *(15)* to see people breathe with their mouths rather than through their noses. If you take a minute and look at the people around you, you may easily find somebody whose mouth is always slightly open for breathing. In order to take a good deep *(20)* breath, you must first breathe out all the air in your lungs. By doing so, you naturally breathe in more air. An expert recommends holding your breath for about two seconds between breaths — that is, you exhale for 15 seconds, pause for two seconds *(25)* and breathe in for three seconds. While you are taking a deep breath, to ease your tension, empty your mind of negative thoughts and breathe using your diaphragm. In case your mind wanders off or if you have difficulty focusing, listen to the sound of your own breathing and count *(30)* backwards slowly.

CHECK YOUR COMPREHENSION

a. Answer the following questions.
   1. What is stress?
   2. What can happen to your body as a result of stress?
   3. What is a quick way to release stress?
   4. How many seconds should you exhale for?
   5. What can you do to help yourself focus?

b. Correct the following statements.
   1. In everyday life, there is no stress.
   2. Only negative events cause stress.
   3. Stress in itself is very dangerous.
   4. Most people breathe through their noses, not their mouths.
   5. An expert recommends taking shallow breaths.

QUESTIONS AND ANSWERS — Symptoms Related to Mental Fatigue

Student A (Student B, see page 98)

a. Memorize and ask these questions to Student B and complete your chart.
1. What seems to be (Edward)'s problem?
2. What can be a cause of stress to (Edward)?
3. What does (Edward) do to relax?
4. What kind of person is (Edward)?

Name	Problem/Symptom	Cause of Stress	Way to Relax	Personality
Edward		finances		tolerant
Frank	anemia		listens to music	
George		school exams		stubborn
Harry	shortness of breath		plays games	
You				
Partner				

b. Answer the following questions.
1. Who seems to be under a great deal of stress? Why?
2. Who has the best stress management strategy?

28

Unit 4
Stress Management — Don't Let it Get to You!

MODEL DIALOGUE — JIGSAW LISTENING

Student A (Student B, see page 99)

Listen, repeat and fill in the blanks.

A: Hey _____. How _____ you today?
B: Oh, hi, Jane, I'm just not myself today.
A: What's the _____?
B: I'm overwhelmed with schoolwork.
A: You do seem a little _____ _____.
B: I have too much to do and too little time.
A: If you _____ some help, I'm right _____. Just _____ me _____ what I can _____.
B: Thanks. It's just something I have to deal with myself. Thank you for asking, though.
A: The best thing is to _____ it _____. Do one thing _____ a _____ by making _____ _____.
B: Yeah, I should, but I'm just too busy to even make plans.
A: That sounds _____. I've _____ in that _____ before.
B: So, how did you manage your stress then?

ACT OUT THE DIALOGUE

Work with your partner.
1. Silently and quickly read and remember one line at a time.
2. Look up at your partner and speak while keeping eye contact.
3. Change roles and practice again by replacing some parts with your own words.

FACT DICTATION

Here are some nice things to say to people stressed out. Listen and fill in the blanks.

1. That _____ _____ _____ tough.
2. If you want to talk about it, I'm here; come on, _____ _____ _____ _____ .
3. Though I may not _____ _____ _____ , I'll be _____ _____ _____ .
4. I believe _____ does _____ all _____ .
5. Let _____ _____ _____ past and move _____ _____ your life.
6. We all need to just stop and _____ _____ _____ every now and _____ .
7. Everything will _____ _____ OK. Don't _____ _____ over it.

IN YOUR OWN WORDS

a. List three common causes of stress in college life.
   •   •   •

b. Name three effective ways to manage stress.
   •   •   •

CRITICAL THINKING — False dichotomy

Explain what is wrong with the following statement:

When are you going to accept my offer? It's now or never. If you don't accept my offer, you'll never succeed.

Unit 5

Skin — Beauty is Only Skin Deep

MATCHING

Match the words (1-9) with the correct definitions (a-i).

1. ___ wrinkles
2. ___ plump
3. ___ sag
4. ___ dilate
5. ___ permanently
6. ___ discolor
7. ___ chilly
8. ___ foremost
9. ___ eventually

a. being cold enough to make you feel uncomfortable
b. to become wider, larger; to enlarge
c. to make something change color, so that it looks unattractive
d. after some time has passed, or after a lot of things have happened
e. the best or most important
f. always, or for a very long time; forever
g. slightly fat in a fairly pleasant way
h. to hang down or bend in the middle
i. lines on your face and skin that you get when you are old

GAP-FILL EXERCISE

Complete the sentences with the words from MATCHING.

1. Drinking too much coffee will _____ your teeth.
2. The tomatoes were big and _____ .
3. The technician _____ found the source of the problem.
4. The old bed _____ s in the middle.
5. That chemical is used to _____ the eyes for eye examinations.
6. "It's _____ in the mornings and hot in the afternoons."

———*Tom Dean, singer*

7. The accident left him _____ disabled.

31

VOCABULARY ANALOGIES

Analogies show how words are related. For example, LISTEN is to SOUND as SEE is to SIGHT.

1. **Wet** is to **drier** as **thick** is to _____.
   a. thinner   **b.** thicker   **c.** thin
2. **Lines** is to **wrinkles** as **spots** is to _____.
   a. surface   **b.** freckles   **c.** faces
3. **Sag** is to **drop** as **pierce** is to _____.
   a. spring back   **b.** take away   **c.** go into
4. **Temperature** is to **fever** as **water** is to _____.
   a. moisture   **b.** position   **c.** dry
5. **Protein** is to **collagen** as **expression** is to _____.
   a. worries   **b.** face   **c.** frown
6. **Hard** is to **leathery** as **soft** is to _____.
   a. plump   **b.** leather   **c.** bags
7. **Wide** is to **dilated** as **red** is to _____.
   a. permanent   **b.** flushed   **c.** wrinkled

BEFORE YOU LISTEN

Listen for answers to the following questions.
1. What makes people look old?
2. How many enemies to skin are there?
3. Which is the major cause of trouble?

LISTEN

Close the textbook and take notes about the key information.

Some people look young for their age while others look older than they actually are. The major difference comes from their skin condition. Our body is covered with skin, which determines *(5)* how we look to people around us. With age, our skin becomes thinner and drier, we get wrinkles, and freckles turn into brown age spots. Although some signs of aging are just a fact of nature, there *(10)* is something you can do to look the best for your age by knowing what factors speed up your skin's aging process.

The first and foremost enemy of your skin is sunlight. Ultraviolet (UV) rays pierce our skin's surface and break down collagen. Sun-weakened skin becomes loose, wrinkled, and leathery. The skin sags and cannot spring back as easily as it could when you were young. If you look at your skin color under your arms near the armpit and compare that skin to your facial skin, you will see what the sun has done. UV rays have discolored the facial skin but not the back of your arms. *(15)*

Going out in cold weather is not good for your skin either. Low temperatures and chilly winds take away moisture (from your face) and make your skin very dry. *(20)*

A lack of sleep shows up on people's faces with dark circles and bags under their eyes. Also, sleeping in the same position every night shows in faces. Sleeping face down on the pillow eventually causes wrinkles on the forehead, and sleeping on your side leads to so-called "sleep lines" on the chin and cheeks. *(25)*

Too much stress and too many worries make you frown so much that your facial muscles remember that movement and the lines become wrinkles.

Alcohol dilates blood vessels and increases blood flow near the skin. If you drink heavily, the blood vessels in your face can be permanently damaged and your face becomes red and you always look flushed. *(30)*

Tobacco smoke, whether you smoke or spend time with smokers, damages your skin very quickly. It causes dry skin and wrinkles because it takes away Vitamin C, which keeps skin plump and moist.

CHECK YOUR COMPREHENSION

a. Answer the following questions.
1. As we become older, what happens to our skin?
2. What is the biggest threat to your skin?
3. What two things indicate a lack of sleep?
4. What does too much alcohol do to the blood vessels?
5. What are the benefits of Vitamin C?

b. Correct the following statements.
1. Sunlight is good for our skin.
2. High temperatures and chilly winds add moisture.
3. "Sleep lines" are dark circles and bags under the eyes.
4. Alcohol decreases blood flow near the skin.
5. Tobacco smoke damages your skin very slowly.

QUESTIONS AND ANSWERS — Skin Conditions

Student A (Student B, see page 100)

a. Memorize and ask these questions to Student B and complete your chart.
1. What seems to be (Edward)'s problem?
2. Since when has (Edward) had this?
3. What does (Edward) do to prevent the problem?
4. What (medicine) does (Edward) take to treat the symptom?

Name	Problem / Symptom	How did it happen?	Cause(s)	Treatment(s)
Edward	skin rash		eczema (allergy)	
Frank		walked barefoot in a locker room		fungicides
George	pimples		bacteria in the pores	
Harry		spilled a boiling pot on himself		salve / ointment is not good
You				
Partner				

b. Answer the following questions.
1. Whose skin condition can be infectious/contagious/transmitted?
2. Whose condition may take the longest to cure? Why?

34

Unit 5
Skin — Beauty is Only Skin Deep

MODEL DIALOGUE — JIGSAW LISTENING

Student A (Student B, see page 101)

Listen, repeat and fill in the blanks.

A: Hello, Henry. Long time _____ _____. How _____ you _____?

B: Yes, it's been a while, Melinda. I've been OK. You haven't changed a bit.

A: Thank you, I've been _____ _____ lately. What _____ you? Your skin _____ a little red.

B: Well, I was out in the sun too long, playing golf.

A: Is it _____ _____ your skin _____ off?

B: Yes, it really hurts. I put on SPF 15 sunscreen, but maybe too late.

A: That _____. It blocks UV-A. I _____ sunscreen all year _____.

B: No wonder you don't look a day older than when we first met.

A: Thanks. I try to _____ good _____ _____ myself.

B: So, what's the secret to being so healthy? Just the sunscreen?

A: There are a _____ other _____, too!

B: Do tell!

ACT OUT THE DIALOGUE

Work with your partner.
1. Silently and quickly read and remember one line at a time.
2. Look up at your partner and speak while keeping eye contact.
3. Change roles and practice again by replacing some parts with your own words.

35

FACT DICTATION

Here is some useful information. Listen and fill in the blanks.

1. The problem with aging is that _____ of aging and wrinkles _____ _____ by excessive sun exposure.

2. Another problem with aging _____ _____ gravity _____ _____ all skin, _____ the face.

3. A lack of exercise _____ _____ aging. Exercising _____ the blood flowing and _____ your muscles.

4. Facial exercise may be _____ _____ most facial muscles get _____ _____ when we eat, talk, _____ our eyes, smile and _____.

5. A face-lift _____ a surgical procedure _____ _____ reduce facial wrinkles, and eliminate _____ _____ _____ on the face and jaw area.

6. Chemical peeling uses _____ to _____ the texture of facial skin by _____ damaged outer layers.

7. As they _____, "There's more than _____ _____ to skin a _____."

IN YOUR OWN WORDS

a. List three advantages of cosmetic surgery.
   •   •   •

b. Name three disadvantages of cosmetic surgery.
   •   •   •

CRITICAL THINKING — Fallacy of equivocation

Explain what is wrong with the following statement:
   A female friend of mine never leaves home without putting on some makeup. Since she says she likes cosmetics a lot, I think she would like to undergo cosmetic surgery. After all, everyone wants to be more beautiful.

Unit 6

Sports Injuries—RICE is Nice

MATCHING

Match the words (1-8) with the correct definitions (a-h).

1. ___ critical
2. ___ majority
3. ___ avoid
4. ___ prevent
5. ___ bruise
6. ___ swollen
7. ___ tingle
8. ___ inflamed

a. to stay away from something or someone
b. a purple or brown mark on your skin due to fall or hit, etc.
c. important; significant
d. being red and swollen, because of injury or infection
e. most of the people or things in a group
f. to stop something from happening, or stop someone from doing something
g. being bigger than usual, because of illness or injury
h. to have a slight stinging feeling, especially of your skin

GAP-FILL EXERCISE

Complete the sentences with the words from MATCHING.

1. I got a big _____ when I fell on the ice.
2. You should _____ oily foods.
3. My right arm aches and my fingers _____ .
4. His eyes were _____ from crying.
5. The next few games will be _____ for the team.
6. We took actions to _____ a fire from happening.
7. The _____ of the general public knows little about science.

VOCABULARY ANALOGIES

Analogies show how words are related. For example, LISTEN is to SOUND as SEE is to SIGHT.

1. **Use** is to **overuse** as **exert** is to _____.
   a. overpower **b.** overlook **c.** overexert
2. **Twist** is to **sprain** as **stretch** is to _____.
   a. strain **b.** pull **c.** joint
3. **Bruising** is to **bleeding** as **overstretching** is to _____.
   a. damage **b.** fibers **c.** pulled muscles
4. **Strain** is to **muscles** as **contusion** is to _____.
   a. bruising **b.** blood **c.** vessels
5. **Brown** is to **ground** as **red** is to _____.
   a. inflammation **b.** pain **c.** symptoms
6. **Wrap** is to **bandage** as **support** is to _____.
   a. bone **b.** splint **c.** broken
7. **Arm** is to **sling** as **leg** is to _____.
   a. crutches **b.** pillow **c.** ice pack

BEFORE YOU LISTEN

Listen for answers to the following questions.
1. When do people injure themselves?
2. How many categories of injuries are there?
3. How many steps are there in treating sports injuries?

LISTEN

Close the textbook and take notes about the key information.

Countless sports injuries happen every year worldwide although 30-50% of these injuries can be prevented. Have you ever hurt yourself when playing sports with friends in the schoolyard or *(5)* during friendly pick-up games in the park? Injuries are more likely to occur in these situations because protective gear and rules are often overlooked. Falls and overexertion cause most *(10)* injuries. The body parts that are most often injured are arms, elbows and

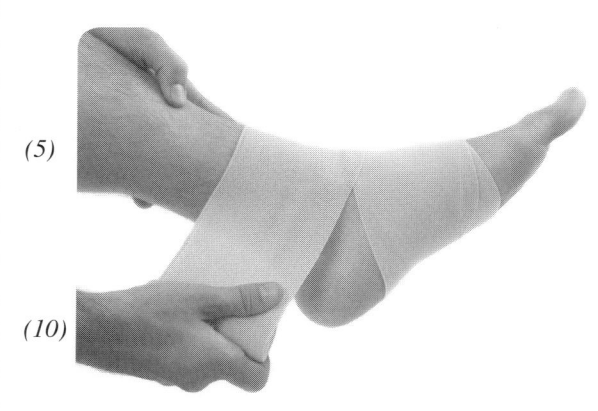

Unit 6

Sports Injuries — RICE is Nice

fingers.

    There are three kinds of injuries: direct injuries, indirect injuries and overuse injuries. A direct injury occurs as a result of contact with another player, an object or the ground. Indirect injury is caused by physical impact without direct contact. Overuse injury results from continual impact on a bone or a tendon, the band connecting a bone and muscle. *(15)*

    The majority of these injuries fall into the following three categories:
1. Strains, or pulled muscles, are tears of muscle fibers as a result of overstretching. *(20)*
2. Sprains are twists in a joint, which tear ligament, the connective tissue between bones in a joint.
3. Bruising, or contusion, is damage to small blood vessels, which causes bleeding in tissues.

    Regardless of how and where strains, sprains and bruises occur, inflammation is the first stage in the natural healing process. In most cases, this stage lasts around five days. With inflammation, the injured area becomes painful, swollen, hot, red and is of limited or no use. To treat these symptoms, the "RICE" method, spelled R-I-C-E, is often used. *(25)*
Rest—You must rest the injured body part before doing anything else and avoid painful movements. The first 24 to 48 hours is critical. You may need a splint, sling or crutches. *(30)*
Ice—Put an ice pack on the area for 20 minutes every three to four hours for the first 48 hours. However, be careful not to ice for more than 20 minutes at a time. This can cause tissue damage! **Compression**—Wrap the area with a bandage. It should fit firmly, but not too tightly. If your fingers or toes turn blue or begin to tingle, the bandage is too tight!
Elevation—Keep your injured body part higher than your heart. If your arm or leg is injured, you can put a pillow or two under it when sleeping. *(35)*

CHECK YOUR COMPREHENSION

a. Answer the following questions.
1. What percentage of sports injuries can be prevented?
2. What body parts are injured most often?
3. What are the three kinds of injuries?
4. How long does the first stage of the healing process last?
5. How often should you use an ice pack during the first two days?

b. Correct the following statements.
1. Falls and overexertion cause the least sports injuries.
2. Strains are twists in joints.
3. Inflammation usually lasts around 48 hours.
4. The first 24 hours is critical.
5. You should keep your injured body part lower than your heart.

QUESTIONS AND ANSWERS — At a Hospital Reception

Student A (Student B, see page 102)

a. Memorize and ask these questions to Student B and complete your chart.
1. How did (Fumie) (sprain) her (finger)?
2. What happened to (Fumie) yesterday?
3. When did (Fumie) (sprain) her (finger)?

- She was (playing) (ping-pong).
- She (sprained) her (finger).
- It happened (yesterday).

Beth:
What? ....
playing tennis
last night

Fumie:
What? *sprained finger*
How? *playing ping-pong*
When? *yesterday*

Chris:
What? ....
boxing
When? ....

broken toes
How? ....
When? ....

sprained ankle
How? ....
three days ago

torn ligaments
How? ....
When? ....

b. Answer the following questions.
1. Who has the most severe injury?
2. Whose injury is the most recent?
3. What sport may cause injuries most often?

Unit 6

Sports Injuries — RICE is Nice

MODEL DIALOGUE — JIGSAW LISTENING

Student A (Student B, see page 103)

Listen, repeat and fill in the blanks.

A: Hi, John. Have you _____ Jim recently? I haven't seen him _____ for a while.

B: Yes, as a matter of fact. I saw him the other day, walking on crutches and wearing a sling.

A: A sling and _____? What _____?

B: He hurt himself playing football over the weekend.

A: You _____ _____ or rugby?

B: American football, actually.

A: How _____ that _____?

B: He said he fell in the middle of the field and three other guys fell right on top of him.

A: Ouch! That _____ very _____. Where _____ he _____, St. Luke's Hospital?

B: Yes, and he got stitches on his forehead, too. Hey, speak of the devil, here he comes right now.

A: Hey, there's the football _____! Who _____ the game, Jim? No, _____, are you _____ right?

ACT OUT THE DIALOGUE

Work with your partner.
1. Silently and quickly read and remember one line at a time.
2. Look up at your partner and speak while keeping eye contact.
3. Change roles and practice again by replacing some parts with your own words.

41

FACT DICTATION

Here are some interesting facts. Listen and fill in the blanks.

1. The _____ _____ of injury management _____ to correctly _____ the injury.
2. An injury like a _____ or a _____ muscle _____ not visible.
3. However, a _____ knee or a cut hand _____ _____.
4. In many _____, pain is the _____ _____ of injury.
5. The second step of the _____ is the _____ _____ of the injury.
6. The third and _____ step is _____ _____ the sport.
7. However, some athletes _____ too quickly and _____ the injury much worse.

IN YOUR OWN WORDS

a. List three ways to prevent sports injuries.
-
-
-

b. Describe three injuries you have had. When did they happen? How did they happen?
-
-
-

CRITICAL THINKING — Biased data

Explain what is wrong with the following statement:
   More people are injured every year playing basketball than bungee jumping. Therefore, bungee jumping is safer than playing basketball.

42

Review Unit 1-6

TOEHM
(Test of English for Health Matters)

Part 1 Picture Descriptions (Vocabulary Review)

You will hear three short statements. Look at the picture and choose the statement that best describes what you see in the picture.

1.

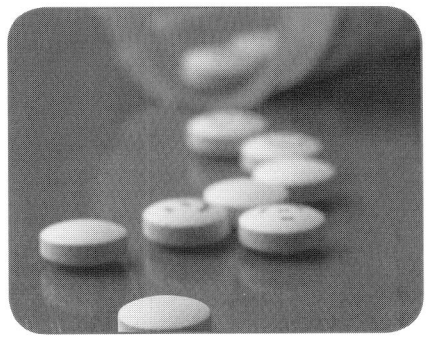

A B C

2.

A B C

3.

A B C

4.

A B C

43

Part 2 — Question - Response

You will hear a question followed by three responses. You are to choose the best response to each question.

1. Mark your answer.　　A　B　C
2. Mark your answer.　　A　B　C
3. Mark your answer.　　A　B　C
4. Mark your answer.　　A　B　C
5. Mark your answer.　　A　B　C
6. Mark your answer.　　A　B　C

Part 3 — Short Conversations

You will hear short conversations between two people. You will read three questions about each conversation followed by three answers. You are to choose the best answer to each question.

1. Where most likely does the woman work?
   A. At the registration desk
   B. At the information stand
   C. At the nurses' station

2. What would the man like to do?
   A. Keep a promise
   B. Make a room reservation
   C. Reschedule an appointment

3. What most likely was the man's earlier problem?
   A. A sprain
   B. A toothache
   C. A pulled muscle

4. Who most likely are the speakers?
   A. Dietitians
   B. Pharmacists
   C. Physicians

5. What problem are the speakers discussing?
   A. Capable doctors
   B. Confused patients
   C. A difficult diagnosis

6. What seems to be the man's problem?
   A. He couldn't identify the correct journal.
   B. His symptoms will not go away.
   C. He doesn't understand English well.

Review Unit 1-6

TOEHM (Test of English for Health Matters)

Part 4 Short Talk

You will hear a short talk (announcement, advertisement, report, speech, etc.). You will read three questions about the talk followed by three answers. Select the best answer to each question.

1. Who is speaking?
   A. A doctor
   B. A radio broadcaster
   C. A school counselor

2. What is included in the program?
   A. An hour-long exam
   B. Tips on stress management
   C. Signs and symptoms of diabetes

3. From whom should people get more information?
   A. From the Council
   B. From the Counselor
   C. From the Medical School

Part 5 Incomplete Sentences

A word or phrase is missing in each of the sentences below. Select the best answer to complete the sentence.

1. English is the key necessary to _____ information in the global network.
   A. assist
   B. assess
   C. access

2. To avoid being in a chronic _____ of jet lag you should keep the same sleep schedule seven days a week.
   A. state
   B. feel
   C. air

3. Without English, you _____ a shortage of information and may be trapped in the world of the unknown.
   A. face
   B. forehead
   C. forearm

4. Learn relaxation skills _____ proper breathing, meditation and stretching your muscles.
   A. including
   B. besides
   C. even when

5. Ultraviolet (UV) _____ pierce the skin's surface and break down collagen.
   A. rays
   B. light
   C. glitter

6. You cannot _____ a lack of sleep on one day by sleeping late on another day.
   A. get rid of
   B. take advantage of
   C. make up for

7. Strains are also colloquially known as _____ muscles.
   A. pull
   B. pulling
   C. pulled

8. Alcohol dilates blood vessels and increases blood _____ near the skin.
   A. flow
   B. vessels
   C. type

9. We'll cross that bridge _____ we come to it.
   A. over
   B. when
   C. together

10. The _____ system protects us from diseases.
    A. digestive
    B. circulatory
    C. immune

11. Currently available therapies for the allergy focus on symptom _____.
    A. surgery
    B. pharmacy
    C. relief

12. Symptoms of strain include pain, stiffness, inflammation and _____ around the strained muscle.
    A. injury
    B. sprain
    C. bruising

Review Unit 1-6

TOEHM (Test of English for Health Matters)

Part 6 Reading Comprehension : Text 1

Read the text (article, letter, advertisement, webpage) followed by four questions. Select the best answer to each question.

Use Medications Safely

When we become sick, we can go and see a doctor and receive a prescription from him or her. We can also self-diagnose and buy an over-the-counter medicine at a drugstore. Here is something you have to remember when buying medicines. Check whether the medicines and herbal medicines that you buy are safe to take along with any prescription medicine you are taking. This is because seemingly different medicines and herbal remedies may well have the same ingredients. Beware that most medicines have two names — the brand name (or trade name) and the ingredient name (or approved name). Different pharmaceutical companies have different brand names for their drugs, which may contain the same ingredients. For example, imagine "Buffaron" and "Tylaryn," two fictional medicines. Both of these trade names are spelled very differently, but they both contain the same ingredient called "aspirin," which is an approved name. If you take two or more medicines without knowing their ingredients, you could end up taking more than the recommended daily dose of a drug. Also, some medicines can interfere with each other; the over-the-counter medicine you are taking may prevent the prescribed medicines from working properly. So, always check with your pharmacist that any medicines or herbal remedies you buy are safe to take with your prescribed medicines.

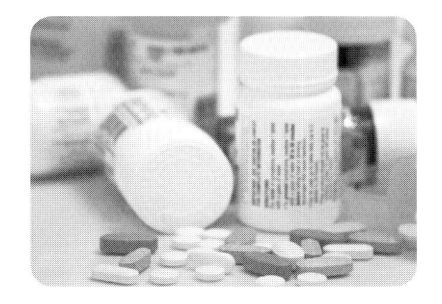

1. Who writes prescriptions?
   A. Pharmacists
   B. Doctors
   C. Patients

2. What may differ most?
   A. Trade names
   B. Ingredient names
   C. Approved names

3. What is NOT mentioned as a risk?
   A. Drug overdose
   B. Taking interfering drugs
   C. Misspelling drug names

4. What is true of herbal remedies?
   A. They are as effective as any medicines.
   B. They have different approved names.
   C. They may not be safe to take with other medicines.

47

Part 7 Reading Comprehension : Text 2

Read the text (article, letter, advertisement, webpage) followed by four questions. Select the best answer to each question.

---

71 piece Sports First Aid Kit (SM-885).

A large first aid kit with compartmental organizers developed specifically for sports activities. Contains the American Medical Association First Aid Guide, tweezers, scissors, cold compresses, latex-free elastic bandages, gauze, antiseptics and a variety of essential first aid supplies.

This all-purpose Sports First Aid kit is suitable for all sports. Whatever you play – badminton, baseball, basketball, bowling, cheer-leading, dance, field hockey, football, golf, gymnastics, hockey, lacrosse, martial arts, rugby, sailing, self defense, skating, soccer, softball, swimming, table tennis, tennis, track, volleyball & wrestling!

Act now! Order by phone and pay just $19.99—savings of 34%. Limited time offer—while supplies last.

Suggested Retail $29.99

---

1. What does SM-855 include?
   A. Cloth for dressing wounds
   B. Personal organizers
   C. Sports gear

2. How much is the kit in drugstores and sports stores?
   A. $19.99
   B. $29.99
   C. $34.99

3. What sport is NOT listed?
   A. Basketball
   B. Rugby
   C. Fencing

4. How long does the sale last?
   A. Until all the kits are sold
   B. Up until the deadline
   C. Until the end of time

Unit 7

Personality— You Need to Chill Out!

MATCHING

Match the words (1-8) with the correct definitions (a-h).

1. ___ impatient
2. ___ honk
3. ___ conduct
4. ___ type
5. ___ tense
6. ___ workaholic
7. ___ aggressive
8. ___ behavior

a. behaving in an angry, threatening way, as if fighting
b. the things that a person or animal does
c. to carry out a particular activity or process
d. a subdivision of a particular kind of thing
e. to make a loud noise
f. annoyed because of delays, someone else's mistakes, etc.
g. feeling worried, uncomfortable, and unable to relax
h. someone who works a lot and has no time to do anything else

GAP-FILL EXERCISE

Complete the sentences with the words from MATCHING.

1. He is a strong and _____ rugby player.
2. He spends all his time making music. He's a _____ .
3. The researcher will _____ a study next month.
4. The happy mother praised her son's _____ .
5. The angry driver _____ ed his horn at me.
6. I'm always _____ before making speeches.
7. She was _____ and didn't want to wait.

49

VOCABULARY ANALOGIES

Analogies show how words are related. For example, LISTEN is to SOUND as SEE is to SIGHT.

1. **Cardiologists** is to **hearts** as **psychologists** is to _____.
   a. workaholics   **b.** characteristics   **c.** novels
2. **Estimated** is to **numbers** as **calculated** is to _____.
   a. findings   **b.** papers   **c.** figures
3. **Impatient** is to **patient** as **tense** is to _____.
   a. relaxed   **b.** published   **c.** learned
4. **Hostile** is to **kind** as **aggressive** is to _____.
   a. unkind   **b.** friendly   **c.** violent
5. **Competitive** is to **pushy** as **buzzword** is to _____.
   a. behavior   **b.** result   **c.** slogan
6. **Suffer** is to **from** as **slow** is to _____.
   a. up   **b.** down   **c.** in
7. **Meet** is to **deadlines** as **feel** is to _____.
   a. pressures   **b.** personalities   **c.** diseases

BEFORE YOU LISTEN

Listen for answers to the following questions.

1. What was discovered in the 1950s?
2. Which type of people are in more danger of getting sick?
3. What can be changed and what cannot be changed?

LISTEN

Close the textbook and take notes about the key information.

What are the factors of heart disease? In the 1950s, they used to say diet and cholesterol until Dr. Meyer Friedman and Dr. Ray Rosenman, cardiologists and heart specialists, *(5)* published scientific papers describing a link between personality and heart attacks.

What was the connection? They conducted a nine-year study observing *(10)* more than 3,000 people between the ages of 35 and 59 years old. They

Unit 7
Personality — You Need to Chill Out!

estimated that people with certain personalities are twice as likely to suffer from coronary heart diseases as other people. In 1974, based on their findings, they wrote the well-known book, *Type A Behavior and Your Heart*. This book explains that highly motivated (15) people who feel time pressures are more likely to have heart problems. These people are said to have Type A Behavior or a "Type A personality." As a result of this book, the term "Type A personality" became a buzzword in the United States.

What are Type A and Type B Behaviors? Type A Behavior Pattern, commonly known as "Type A personality," is a set of personality characteristics. These people (20) can be very tense and impatient. For example, they are likely to honk their car horns in frustration while in traffic jams and complain to salesclerks. Also, they can become hostile and aggressive easily. At work, these people are competitive workaholics who often feel it necessary to multi-task in order to meet deadlines. On the other hand, Type B Behavior Pattern is the opposite of Type A Behavior Pattern. These people are relaxed, (25) patient and friendly.

Unfortunately, we cannot change our personalities, but we can change our behavior patterns. In the 1980s, Dr. Friedman found that when Type A people learned how to slow down and relax, the risk for heart attacks could be dramatically reduced. He recommended Type A people do some exercises to become more like Type B people. For (30) example, he recommended that people force themselves to slow down by driving in the slow lane instead of the passing lane and by choosing the longest checkout line in the supermarket. He also encouraged people to read classic novels and literature.

CHECK YOUR COMPREHENSION

a. Answer the following questions.
  1. Who are Dr. Friedman and Dr. Rosenman?
  2. What was the name of their 1974 book?
  3. What are some things that Type A people do?
  4. What did Dr. Friedman find in the 1980s?
  5. What should Type A people do?

b. Correct the following statements.
  1. "Type A personality" became a buzzword in Argentina.
  2. Type A people cannot meet deadlines because they are lazy.
  3. Type A people are relaxed, patient and friendly.
  4. With hard work, we can change our personalities.
  5. As an exercise, Type B people should drive in the fast lane instead of the slow lane.

QUESTIONS AND ANSWERS — Behavior Test

Student A (Student B, see page 104)

Partner A asks the odd-numbered questions. Check your partner's answers in the boxes ☐ and your answers in the circles ○.

1. How quickly do you usually speak?
   - ☐ Faster than most people ○ a
   - ☐ Average speed ○ b
   - ☐ Slower than most people ○ c

2. _____?
   - ☐ Take action immediately ○ a
   - ☐ Think and then take action ○ b
   - ☐ Wait for the problem to fix itself ○ c

3. How quickly do you finish school assignments?
   - ☐ Before all of your classmates ○ a
   - ☐ Before most of your classmates ○ b
   - ☐ Just on time ○ c
   - ☐ Late ○ d

4. _____?
   - ☐ Faster than most people ○ a
   - ☐ Average speed ○ b
   - ☐ Slower than most people ○ c

5. How often do you finish other people's sentences?
   - ☐ Often ○ a
   - ☐ Sometimes ○ b
   - ☐ Almost never ○ c

6. _____?
   - ☐ Very important ○ a
   - ☐ Sometimes important ○ b
   - ☐ Not important ○ c

7. How often are you late for appointments?
   - ☐ Almost always ○ a
   - ☐ Sometimes ○ b
   - ☐ Almost never ○ c
   - ☐ Never ○ d

8. _____?
   - ☐ Very important ○ a
   - ☐ Sometimes important ○ b
   - ☐ Not important ○ c

9. How do your friends describe you?
   - ☐ Always hardworking and serious ○ a
   - ☐ Sometimes hardworking and serious ○ b
   - ☐ Rarely hardworking and serious ○ c
   - ☐ Lazy and not serious ○ d

10. _____?
    - ☐ Sleep ○ a
    - ☐ Watch TV ○ b
    - ☐ Go shopping ○ c
    - ☐ Clean your room ○ d

11. Do you use a schedule book?
    - ☐ Never ○ a
    - ☐ Sometimes ○ b
    - ☐ Always ○ c

12. _____?
    - ☐ Two weeks ahead ○ a
    - ☐ One week ahead ○ b
    - ☐ A day before ○ c
    - ☐ Don't study! ○ d

The scoring guide is on page 103
If your score is less than 150, you have a Type B personality.
If your score is more than 150, you have a Type A personality.

Unit 7
Personality — You Need to Chill Out!

MODEL DIALOGUE — JIGSAW LISTENING

Student A (Student B, see page 105)

Listen, repeat and fill in the blanks.

A: Hey, Mike, _____ are you _____?
B: Oh, hi, Sue. I'm taking a personality test.
A: A personality test? You've _____ to _____ kidding! What _____ you fail and _____ _____ personality?
B: Very funny. Everyone has a personality. Actually, this particular test is quite fascinating.
A: What's _____ _____ about it?
B: Well, this test can determine whether I am a Type A or Type B person.
A: Aha! You don't _____ a test. I can _____ you _____. You are a _____ Type A person.
B: I am?
A: Yes, you are _____ and too _____-oriented.
B: Ouch! You know me too well. Thanks for being painfully honest!
A: Sorry to be so _____. I'm too _____ sometimes. Maybe I'm a _____ Type A, too!
B: That's okay. I'm trying to become more of a Type B person. I've started drawing to help me relax.
A: That's a good _____. Why don't you _____ listening to _____ music, too?
B: Thanks. I'll give it a try. In a few weeks, I'll be a new person.

ACT OUT THE DIALOGUE

Work with your partner.
1. Silently and quickly read and remember one line at a time.
2. Look up at your partner and speak while keeping eye contact.
3. Change roles and practice again by replacing some parts with your own words.

FACT DICTATION

Here are some tips for relaxing your mind. Listen and fill in the blanks.

1. Do not be _____ by things you have _____ _____ _____.

2. Quit _____ if you can't _____ what will _____ or _____ _____ _____ it.

3. How you _____ the situation is more important than _____ the _____ _____.

4. Situations _____. Everything is _____ _____ _____ of flux.

5. Keep _____ yourself _____ you have _____ than what _____ don't _____.

6. Build your hopes _____ _____ _____ in life, rather than _____ _____ _____ _____.

7. After all, you have _____ _____ _____. What _____ do you want?

IN YOUR OWN WORDS

a. What are three Type A things that you do?
- • • •

b. What are three Type B things that you do?
- • • •

CRITICAL THINKING — False dichotomy

Explain what is wrong with the following statement:
There are only two types of people in the world: selfish people and unselfish people. When Bill is nice to me, he must have a hidden agenda because he is a selfish person.

Unit 8

Nutrition— Nutritious is Delicious

MATCHING

Match the words (1-9) with the correct definitions (a-i).
1. ___ protein
2. ___ mill
3. ___ consist
4. ___ kernel
5. ___ carbohydrate
6. ___ refine
7. ___ nutrient
8. ___ texture
9. ___ poultry

a. a substance which consists of oxygen, carbon and hydrogen
b. to be formed from two or more things or people
c. the part of a nut or seed inside the shell or some fruits
d. a small machine for crushing coffee or pepper; grinder
e. a chemical or food needed for plants or animals to live
f. birds such as chickens and ducks that are kept on farms
g. natural substances that exist in food such as meat, eggs and beans, necessary for the body to grow and remain strong
h. to improve a method, plan, system, etc. by making gradually slight changes
i. the way a surface or material feels when you touch it

GAP-FILL EXERCISE

Complete the sentences with the words from MATCHING.
1. The author worked hard to _____ his or her writing style.
2. Protein is an example of an organic _____ .
3. Silk has a very smooth _____ .
4. Eggs are an excellent source of _____ .
5. Many people use a _____ to grind their coffee beans.
6. Birds kept for meat, eggs and feathers are called _____ .

55

VOCABULARY ANALOGIES

Analogies show how words are related. For example, LISTEN is to SOUND as SEE is to SIGHT.

1. **Nutrition** is to **protein** as **grains** is to _____.
   a. wheat   **b**. meat   **c**. beans
2. **Carbohydrates** is to **rice** as **fiber** is to _____.
   a. zinc   **b**. oats   **c**. iron
3. **Barley** is to **wheat** as **soybean** is to _____.
   a. pumpkin   **b**. mango   **c**. azuki-bean
4. **Refined** is to **fine** as **pureed** is to _____.
   a. smooth   **b**. pure   **c**. liquid
5. **Rough** is to **textures** as **dark** is to _____.
   a. lives   **b**. vitamins   **c**. colors
6. **Poultry** is to **chickens** as **vegetables** is to _____.
   a. yams   **b**. nectarines   **c**. cantaloupes
7. **Kernel** is to **core** as **consist** is to _____.
   a. be processed   **b**. be made up   **c**. be called

BEFORE YOU LISTEN

Listen for answers to the following questions.
1. What do you have to do to live a healthy life?
2. How many groups of food are there?
3. What are examples of these food groups?

LISTEN

Close the textbook and take notes about the key information.

We are what we eat. Our body is made of what we have eaten. We all eat to live, but some people eat smarter. Let's find out how to have a healthy diet. In order to get the nutrition needed *(5)* for the body, we must eat foods from each of the four food groups. They are 1. grains, 2. fruits and vegetables, 3. milk products and 4. meat and beans.

The first group, grains, is *(10)* important because it gives your body carbohydrates, iron, fiber and other

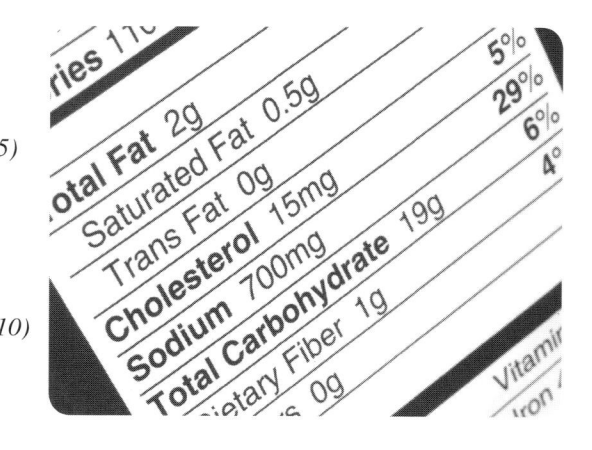

Unit 8
Nutrition — Nutritious is Delicious

important elements. This group includes foods made from wheat, rice, oats, cornmeal, barley or any other cereal grain. Grains fall into two subgroups, whole grains and refined grains. Whole grains are usually brown in color and contain the whole grain seed called *(15)* the kernel. Whole grains are more nutritious than refined grains. Flours made with refined grains have finer textures and longer shelf lives than flours made with whole grains, but have less fiber, iron and other vitamins because they have had the bran and germ removed from the kernel in the milling process.

The second group consists of fruits and vegetables, which are important sources *(20)* for vitamins and fiber. Generally, the darker the color of vegetables, the more nutrients they have. For example, dark green vegetables such as spinach and broccoli as well as some orange vegetables such as carrots, squash, pumpkin, sweet potatoes and yams have more nutrients than vegetables like corn and onions. Orange colored fruits like apricots, cantaloupes, mangoes, nectarines, papayas and peaches are as nutritious as orange *(25)* vegetables. Dried fruit and pureed fruit are also good for you.

The third group includes milk and milk products like yogurt and cheese. They are rich in calcium and protein. Milk products such as butter, cream cheese and cream have little or no calcium.

The fourth group consists of meat, fish, beans, eggs and nuts. These foods are *(30)* important sources for protein, calcium, iron and zinc. High-fat red meat is less healthy than lean, low-fat meat like poultry or fish, nuts and seeds which have healthy oils.

CHECK YOUR COMPREHENSION

a. Answer the following questions.
   1. What are the food groups?
   2. What are grains an important source of?
   3. What does the second food group consist of?
   4. What milk products have little or no calcium?
   5. Why is the fourth group necessary?

b. Correct the following statements.
   1. There are five food groups.
   2. Refined grains have rougher textures and shorter shelf lives than whole grains.
   3. Dried fruit and pureed fruit are not very good for you.
   4. Yogurt and cheese are not rich in protein.
   5. The fourth group consists of meat, fish, bread, eggs and nuts.

QUESTIONS AND ANSWERS — Dietary Recommendations

Student A (Student B, see page 106)

a. Memorize and ask these questions to Student B and complete your chart.
1. What country is number (1)?
2. How many grams are recommended in (Canada)?
3. How many servings are recommended in (Canada)?

Ranking	Country	Number of Grams	Recommended Servings
1		850	
2	Canada		10 portions of fruits and vegetables
3		720	
4	Greece		3 portions of fruits and 6 portions of vegetables
5		650	
6	Germany		5 portions of fruits and vegetables
7		600	
8	Denmark		3 portions of fruits and 3 portions of vegetables
9		560	
10	United Kingdom		5 portions of fruits and vegetables

b. Answer the following questions.
1. Which country recommends the most vegetables?
2. Which country uses the largest serving size?
3. Which country recommends the least fruits?

Unit 8

Nutrition — Nutritious is Delicious

MODEL DIALOGUE — JIGSAW LISTENING

Student A (Student B, see page 107)

Listen, repeat and fill in the blanks.

A: Lisa, _____ up?
B: Not much, David. I'm just looking at this nutrition guidebook.
A: Nutrition? Where _____ this sudden _____ come from?
B: I saw a documentary about diets last night and I wanted to learn more.
A: What did you _____ _____?
B: Well, I realized that I've been eating too many high-fat foods, things like doughnuts.
A: Me, too. I'm sure it's _____ in _____, but those things _____ so good.
B: That's just the problem.
A: What does the book say we _____ _____ eating _____?
B: Well, we should eat more fruit and vegetables, of course.
A: That's _____! I'm _____ about mangosteens and lychees.
B: You are. Really? Those are a little hard to get sometimes. I'm not a big fan of lychees anyway.
A: How can you _____ like lychees?
B: Lychees are troublesome to eat. I prefer more common fruits like apples and bananas.
A: To _____ his _____, I suppose.

ACT OUT THE DIALOGUE

Work with your partner.
1. Silently and quickly read and remember one line at a time.
2. Look up at your partner and speak while keeping eye contact.
3. Change roles and practice again by replacing some parts with your own words.

FACT DICTATION

Here are some useful tips and interesting facts. Listen and fill in the blanks.

1. Nutritionists _____ that you eat _____ _____ of foods.
2. With a _____ _____ and _____ activity, you can _____ or reduce your weight.
3. Avoid too much sugar. _____ sugars _____ _____.
4. If you drink _____, _____ _____ in moderation.
5. Avoid eating foods that are _____ _____ salt and _____.
6. Your body _____ a _____ of _____ every day.
7. As knowledge about _____ _____ _____, dietary recommendations have _____.
8. Surprisingly, recommendations _____ 100 years ago _____ very _____.

IN YOUR OWN WORDS

a. Name three things that you feel you ought to be eating more of.
-
-
-

b. Name three things that you think you should be eating less of.
-
-
-

CRITICAL THINKING — Appeal to authority

Explain what is wrong with the following statement:

Dr. James Watson, president of the Harvard University Nutrition Scientist Association, said he never drinks milk. Therefore, drinking milk is unhealthy.

Unit 9

Aromatherapy— What's that Smell?

MATCHING

Match the words (1-8) with the correct definitions (a-h).
1. ___ vapor
2. ___ state
3. ___ ailment
4. ___ sense
5. ___ influence
6. ___ aroma
7. ___ fragrance
8. ___ emotion

a. an illness that is not very serious
b. a pleasant smell from spices, cooking, etc.
c. a strong human feeling such as love, hate, or anger
d. a pleasant sweet smell
e. the power to affect the way someone or something develops, behaves, or thinks without using direct force or orders
f. one of the five natural powers of sight, hearing, feeling, taste and smell
g. the physical or mental condition that someone or something is in
h. a mass of very small drops of a liquid which float in the air

GAP-FILL EXERCISE

Complete the sentences with the words from MATCHING.
1. The common cold is often thought as a minor _____.
2. The car was in an unusable _____ after the accident.
3. This freshly baked bread has a very strong _____.
4. Many people enjoy the _____ of roses.
5. Television has a very powerful _____ on young people.
6. Water _____ is the source of humidity.
7. Sight and sound are two of the human body's _____s.

VOCABULARY ANALOGIES

Analogies show how words are related. For example, LISTEN is to SOUND as SEE is to SIGHT.

1. **Inner** is to **outer** as **inhale** is to _____.
   a. breathe **b.** extract **c.** exhale
2. **Therapy** is to **therapeutic** as **mouth** is to _____.
   a. oral **b.** psychological **c.** physical
3. **Perfumes** is to **scent** as **coffee** is to _____.
   a. aroma **b.** cologne **c.** odor
4. **Drink** is to **infusions** as **rub** is to _____.
   a. skin **b.** oil **c.** love
5. **Ailment** is to **illness** as **vapor** is to _____.
   a. bath **b.** taste **c.** steam
6. **Properties** is to **qualities** as **affect** is to _____.
   a. influence **b.** characteristics **c.** fungal
7. **Antibacterial** is to **against** as **misleading** is to _____.
   a. correct **b.** wrong **c.** exact

BEFORE YOU LISTEN

Listen for answers to the following questions.

1. How many senses do people have?
2. How old is aromatherapy?
3. How can oils be used?

LISTEN

Close the textbook and take notes about the key information.

How do we get information? We humans only get information through the five senses — sight, sound, smell, taste and touch. One of the strongest senses affects our inner emotions and *(5)* memory. This is the sense of smell. The instant you smell the aroma of morning coffee, you cannot help waking up and feeling like getting ready to work. For more than 6,000 years, the Chinese, *(10)* Egyptians, Indians, Greeks and Romans have been using pleasant-smelling natural oils in cosmetics, perfumes and drugs. Now the treatment using oils extracted from plants to ease anxiety or minor medical conditions is referred to as "aromatherapy."

The purpose of aromatherapy is to affect a person's mood or health by the use (15) of aroma as a therapeutic tool. However, the word "aroma" in aromatherapy can be misleading because aromatic plant extracts and essential oils are not only inhaled, but they can also be rubbed into the skin, used in baths or even taken orally. For example, it is popular in France to drink herb oil infusions.

Aromatherapy has healing qualities due to physical benefits from the oils and their (20) impacts on our mental state. For example, lavender essential oil can be used to treat skin ailments such as acne and fungal infections. In addition to having antibacterial properties, the pleasant fragrance of lavender has calming and sedative effects.

Although researchers do not know exactly how aromatherapy alters our emotions, they do know that when a person smells something, certain parts of the brain are quickly (25) affected. These parts of the brain influence our physical, mental and emotional state.

Aromatherapy massage as well as aroma baths are popular because in addition to the oil vapors influencing the brain, there are the physical benefits from having a massage or taking a bath. They make you feel relaxed not only physically but also psychologically.

CHECK YOUR COMPREHENSION

a. Answer the following questions.
1. What does the sense of smell affect?
2. How have natural oils been used?
3. How can essential oils be used?
4. What can lavender essential oil treat?
5. Why are aroma baths popular?

b. Correct the following statements.
1. Natural oils have been used around the world for around 600 years.
2. Aromatic plant extracts should not be taken orally.
3. In the United States, it is popular to drink herb oil infusions.
4. Our physical and emotional states influence certain parts of our brains.
5. The sense of smell can affect only our mental health.

QUESTIONS AND ANSWERS — Common Essential Oils

Student A (Student B, see page 108)

a. Memorize and ask these questions to Student B and complete your chart.
1. How is (basil) oil used?
2. What can be used as (an antidepressant)?
3. What can be used to (relieve stress)?

Essential Oil	Uses	
basil oil	· to help concentration	·
black pepper oil	·	· to ease aches and pains
citronella oil	· to repel insects	
clove oil	·	· as an antiseptic
eucalyptus oil	· as an antiseptic	·
geranium oil	·	· as an antiseptic
lavender oil	·	
lemon oil	· to relieve stress	·
rose oil	·	
tea tree oil	· as an antiseptic	·

b. Answer the following questions.
1. Which essential oils can be used as antiseptics?
2. Which essential oil has the most uses?
3. Which essential oil can be used as a disinfectant?

Unit 9

Aromatherapy — What's that Smell?

MODEL DIALOGUE — JIGSAW LISTENING

Student A (Student B, see page 109)

Listen, repeat and fill in the blanks.

A: Ben, do you _____ something?
B: Is it me, Kate? I hope not.
A: No, I don't think _____ you, but what is _____ smell?
B: Maybe it's the air freshener I sprayed a few minutes ago.
A: No, I don't think it's the air _____. That _____ smell _____!
B: (*Sniff, Sniff*) Yeah, you're right. Something stinks. It's kind of moldy even.
A: Have you _____ cooking something with, _____ garlic?
B: No. I haven't cooked for weeks, I'm embarrassed to admit.
A: How can you _____ without _____?
B: Oh, don't get me wrong. I eat, but I just don't cook.
A: When was the _____ time you ate a good, _____, home-cooked _____?
B: Well, last week, I had oregano-flavored lamb shank with a delicious gravy.
A: Well, _____ _____ like you are a _____.
B: Not exactly, but I do like good food. I just never find time to make it!
A: Well, _____ me next time you _____!

ACT OUT THE DIALOGUE

Work with your partner.
1. Silently and quickly read and remember one line at a time.
2. Look up at your partner and speak while keeping eye contact.
3. Change roles and practice again by replacing some parts with your own words.

FACT DICTATION

Here are some interesting facts. Listen and fill in the blanks.

1. Do you know that bergamot is _____ _____ _____ popular essential _____?
2. Were you _____ _____ bergamot is a very _____ insect repellent?
3. Plus, it _____ also _____ _____ the urinary and _____ tracts.
4. In addition, it is _____ for skin _____ _____ by stress.
5. Conditions _____ cold _____ and chicken _____ can be _____ as _____.
6. Not only _____, bergamot _____ used to _____ Earl Grey tea.
7. Also, it _____ often _____ with eucalyptus oil.

IN YOUR OWN WORDS

a. Name fragrances that remind you of each of the four seasons.
- spring
- summer
- autumn
- winter

b. Name three smells that remind you of your childhood.
-
-
-

CRITICAL THINKING — Fallacy of origins

Explain what is wrong with the following statement:
> The word "aromatherapy" originally came from aroma, which means smell. Thus, drinking extracts from aromatic plants is not aromatherapy.

Unit 10

Aging—Forever Young

MATCHING

Match the words (1-8) with the correct definitions (a-h).

1. ___ subject
2. ___ reduction
3. ___ owing to
4. ___ process
5. ___ sedentary
6. ___ lung
7. ___ deteriorate
8. ___ athlete

a. a person who is trained to compete in sports
b. to become worse
c. one of the two organs in your body that you breathe with
d. because of
e. a series of actions that are done to achieve a particular result
f. a decrease in the size, price, or amount of something
g. spending a lot of time sitting down, and not moving or exercising very much
h. a person or animal that is used in a test or experiment

GAP-FILL EXERCISE

Complete the sentences with the words from MATCHING.

1. A person who enjoys sports might become an _____.
2. The _____ of pollution is a priority.
3. Vision _____s as people become older.
4. The manufacturing _____ of computers is complex.
5. The human chest contains two _____s.
6. More than 1,000 _____s participated in the study.
7. An office job is a _____ job.
8. _____ his injury, the player quit the race.

VOCABULARY ANALOGIES

Analogies show how words are related. For example, LISTEN is to SOUND as SEE is to SIGHT.

1. **Researchers** is to **studies** as **athletes** is to _____.
   a. diagnoses   b. competes   c. sports
2. **Subjects** is to **experiment** as **people** is to _____.
   a. study   b. reason   c. cause
3. **Sedentary** is to **sitting** as **active** is to _____.
   a. standing   b. lying   c. moving
4. **Grow** is to **old** as **become** is to _____.
   a. slow   b. doctor   c. record
5. **Heart** is to **beats** as **blood** is to _____.
   a. transfusion   b. circulates   c. pressure
6. **Lungs** is to **oxygen** as **heart** is to _____.
   a. ache   b. blood   c. pulse
7. **Deterioration** is to **worse** as **improvement** is to _____.
   a. good   b. better   c. best

BEFORE YOU LISTEN

Listen for answers to the following questions.
1. What are the differences between young and old people?
2. What happens to old people's hearts?
3. What occurs in old people's lungs?

LISTEN

Close the textbook and take notes about the key information.

What happens to people as they grow old? In the past, many researchers who studied the aging process would say as people age, they become weak and slow. Thus, they have to take short *(5)* and careful steps. However, the subjects in these studies were sedentary, that is people who do little or no exercise.

Recently, researchers have begun to study people who are not sedentary. *(10)* They exercise regularly or even began competing in sports after they were

68

Unit 10
Aging — Forever Young

middle-aged or even older.

These studies have found that people slow down because of two reasons. The first reason is one's heartbeat weakens with age. Throughout one's life, the maximum heart *(15)* rate naturally falls by about seven or eight beats per minute every ten years. This happens to both sedentary and active people. As a result of this reduction in the maximum heart rate, the heart cannot pump as much blood, which carries oxygen throughout the body.

The second reason is that lungs cannot take in as much air. Owing to a slower heart rate and less oxygen in the lungs, less blood goes to the muscles. One researcher found *(20)* that high-level athletes between age 55 and 68 had 10 to 20% less blood flow to their legs than athletes in their 20s.

On the positive side, these studies have also shown that regular exercise can slow down the deterioration of muscle mass and muscle. In addition, older people can continue exercising for long periods of time with near their maximum level of performance. *(25)*

For example, Ed Whitlock, a 73-year-old man, ran a full marathon in 2 hours 54 minutes and 48 seconds in 2004. He broke the first Olympic marathon record that was 2 hours 58 minutes and 50 seconds achieved by Spiridon Louis in 1896.

CHECK YOUR COMPREHENSION

a. Answer the following questions.
1. What did researchers used to say about old people?
2. What are the two reasons why people slow down with age?
3. How much does maximum heart rate decrease every ten years?
4. What have studies shown about regular exercise?
5. Who is Ed Whitlock?

b. Correct the following statements.
1. Sedentary people are very active people who exercise regularly.
2. In the past, most aging studies looked at active people.
3. The maximum heart rate of active people increases with age.
4. More blood flows to older athletes than younger athletes.
5. Ed Whitlock won the first Olympic marathon in 1896.

QUESTIONS AND ANSWERS — Acting Young

Student A (Student B, see page 110)

a. Memorize and ask these questions to Student B and complete your chart.
   1. What is (Alfred)'s height and weight?
   2. What is the percentage of (Alfred)'s body fat?
   3. What exercise does (Alfred) do?
   4. What is (Alfred)'s pulse rate?

Name	Height & Weight	Body Fat Percentage	Exercise	Pulse Rate
Alfred	175 cm 70 kg		badminton	
Benjamin		20%		45 beats per minute
Charlie	180 cm 70 kg		football	
David		25%		55 beats per minute
Ellie	160 cm 47 kg		ballet	
Partner				

b. Answer the following questions.
   1. Which exercise burns the least energy?
   2. Who seems to be the healthiest? Why?
   3. Ten years from now, what will your partner's pulse rate be?

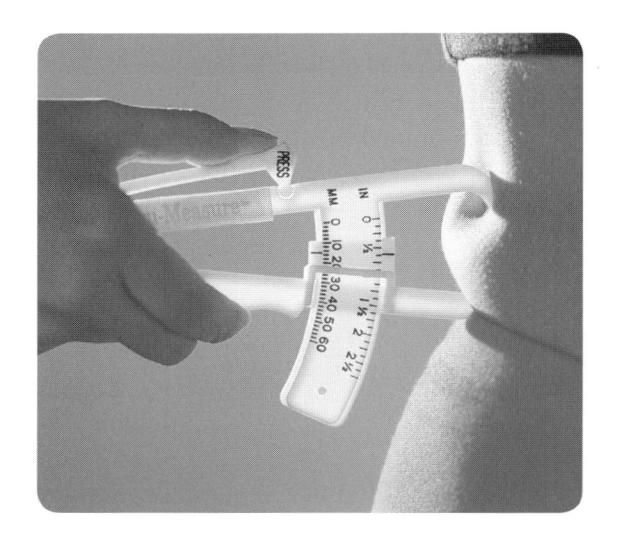

Unit 10
Aging — Forever Young

MODEL DIALOGUE — JIGSAW LISTENING

Student A (Student B, see page 111)

Listen, repeat and fill in the blanks.

A: Rachel, this may _____ like a strange question, but _____ you ever _____ about your _____?
B: No, not really. I'm focused on the here and now.
A: Well then, can you _____ what you'll be _____ 20 years from _____?
B: I'll be in my 40s then. I'll probably be spending my days knitting and gardening. Something calm and boring, I guess.
A: Don't be _____ pessimistic. I'm hoping to _____ earlier than anybody else in my _____.
B: Oh, what will you do then?
A: I want to run _____ all over the _____.
B: Marathons? You mean, like long running races?
A: Exactly, _____ marathons. They _____ them everywhere _____.
B: That's very ambitious. They say, "Youth is not a time of life; it's a state of mind." You can be living proof of that.
A: Yes, I can and _____ can _____. Why don't we _____ a marathon together?
B: What a great idea, Mark! You are so optimistic and full of energy.
A: Yeah, think about _____ we can _____ after retirement, and really all _____ life.
B: Yes, I hadn't thought about it like that. You've just brightened my day. Thanks!

ACT OUT THE DIALOGUE

Work with your partner.
1. Silently and quickly read and remember one line at a time.
2. Look up at your partner and speak while keeping eye contact.
3. Change roles and practice again by replacing some parts with your own words.

71

FACT DICTATION

Here are some interesting facts. Listen and fill in the blanks.

1. The aim of medicine _____ to _____ disease not _____ _____ health.
2. Nobody's life _____ _____ _____ _____ any others'.
3. Given _____, you _____ to _____ _____ for your own health.
4. Exercise _____ and _____ your body _____ _____ _____ _____ you become.
5. Our body is _____ in _____ a _____ that it can _____ itself and _____ itself while _____ used.
6. Developing good _____ from one's youth _____ _____ living a _____ old age.
7. Taken _____, what habits of _____ do you think may _____ good health?

IN YOUR OWN WORDS

a. List three things that cause hypertension (high blood pressure).

b. Name three things that lower blood pressure.

CRITICAL THINKING — An appeal to popularity

Explain what is wrong with the following statement:
   Everybody says that you cannot teach an old dog a new trick. Thus, you cannot learn a foreign language because you're too old to do that.

Unit 11

Acupuncture—On Pins and Needles

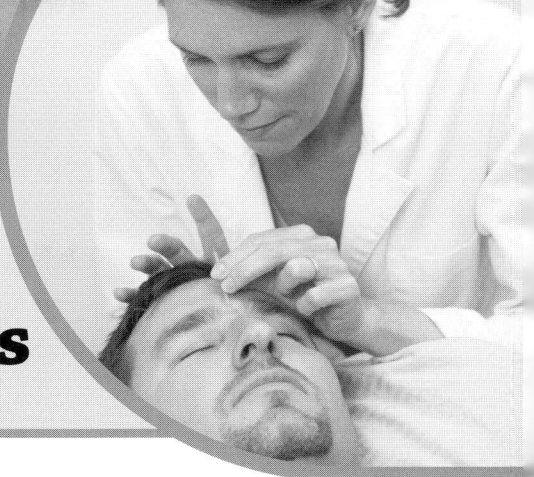

MATCHING

Match the words (1-8) with the correct definitions (a-h).

1. ___ chill
2. ___ diagnose
3. ___ regulate
4. ___ asthma
5. ___ disposable
6. ___ perspiration
7. ___ insert
8. ___ blockage

a. a medical condition that causes difficulties in breathing
b. something that is stopping movement in a narrow place
c. an unpleasant feeling of coldness in the air or in the body
d. to discover what is wrong with someone or something
e. intended to be used once or for a short time and then thrown away
f. to put something inside or into something else
g. liquid that appears on your skin when you are hot or nervous
h. to control an activity or process, especially by rules

GAP-FILL EXERCISE

Complete the sentences with the words from MATCHING.

1. Most _____ products are not good for the environment.
2. A common name for _____ is sweat.
3. _____ is a common respiratory disease.
4. The process is _____d electronically.
5. A _____ in the arteries can cause a heart attack.
6. _____ a coin to make a telephone call.
7. The sick boy had a fever and the _____s.

73

VOCABULARY ANALOGIES

Analogies show how words are related. For example, LISTEN is to SOUND as SEE is to SIGHT.

1. **Back** is to **stomach** as **tender** is to _____.
   a. hard   b. soft   c free
2. **Internal** is to **organs** as **large** is to _____.
   a. pulses   b. allergies   c. intestines
3. **Surface** is to **inside** as **chills** is to _____.
   a. fever   b. status   c. interior
4. **Regulate** is to **control** as **restore** is to _____.
   a. occur   b. fix   c. reflect
5. **Thirst** is to **taste** as **defecation** is to _____.
   a. urination   b. sleep   c. toilet
6. **Wheezing** is to **breathing** as **flowing** is to _____.
   a. meeting   b. moving   c. smelling
7. **Perspiration** is to **sweat** as **menses** is to _____.
   a. pain   b. appetite   c. period

BEFORE YOU LISTEN

Listen for answers to the following questions.
1. What is the name of the healing method?
2. According to Chinese medicine, why do people get sick?
3. How can patients be cured?

LISTEN

Close the textbook and take notes about the key information.

Do you know what healing method has been practiced for more than 2,000 years? The World Health Organization (WHO) has found it useful for more than 40 medical conditions such as allergies, asthma, depression and back pain. This treatment uses needles that are inserted into the body. The answer is "acupuncture."

According to Chinese medicine, health occurs when you have a good balance of   (5)
energy inside of your body, the "Qi," spelled "q-i," pronounced "ki" in Japanese and "chee" in Chinese. The Qi flows through channels called meridians. These channels run up, down, sideways, in all directions all throughout the body. For example, there are six channels in each arm and leg. They are connected to internal organs, including — lungs, intestines, stomach, etc. Acupuncture points are places where the channels meet the body's surface.   (10)

It is believed that a person's health reflects the status of Qi in the body. If the Qi is flowing freely, a person is healthy. If the flow of the Qi is blocked for any reason, illness results. A principle of acupuncture is "no pain, no blockage; no blockage, no pain." *(15)* The purpose of acupuncture is to restore the proper balance and flow of the Qi.

The energy in the channels can be regulated with metal *(20)* needles. Most acupuncturists use disposable stainless steel needles about 3.5 cm in length, of which from 4 mm to 25 mm are inserted. Around six to 12 *(25)* needles are inserted at several spots. The locations of spots depend on the ailment and whether the Qi needs to be warmed, reduced or increased.

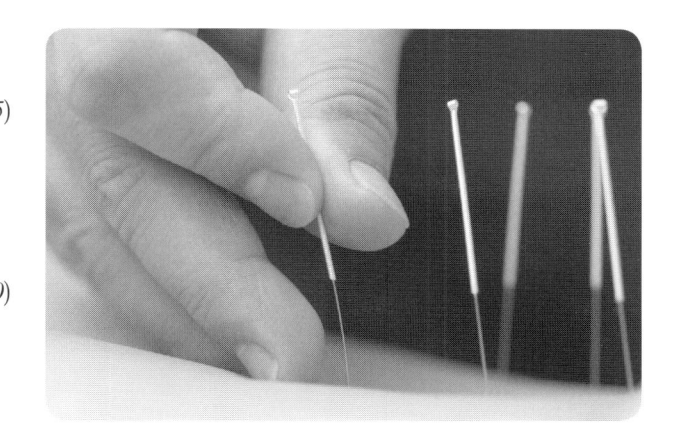

The acupuncturist decides which points to treat by observing and questioning the patient. There are four basic diagnostic methods:
1. Observing the face and the tongue *(30)*
2. Listening for particular sounds like wheezing, and smelling the body
3. Questioning about chills and fever; perspiration; appetite, thirst and taste; defecation and urination; pain; sleep; and menses.
4. Feeling the body for tender points and pulses.

The needles may be inserted for a few seconds or even up to an hour. Although the *(35)* idea of piercing your body with needles sounds painful, once the needles are removed, there are no marks on the skin, and the pain should go away.

CHECK YOUR COMPREHENSION

a. Answer the following questions.
1. How long has acupuncture been practiced?
2. What are some conditions that can be treated?
3. What are acupuncture channels called?
4. What is a principle of acupuncture?
5. How many needles are usually inserted?

b. Correct the following statements.
1. The WHO has found acupuncture useful in treating 2,000 conditions.
2. There are 12 channels in each arm and leg.
3. The energy in the channels is regulated with wooden pins.
4. Needles may be inserted for a few hours.
5. Acupuncture leaves small red marks on the skin.

QUESTIONS AND ANSWERS — Acupuncture Points

Student A (Student B, see page 112)

Point to the acupuncture points on your body and discuss the affected areas with your partner.

1. What is this acupuncture point for?
2. Where is the point for treating (neck pain)?

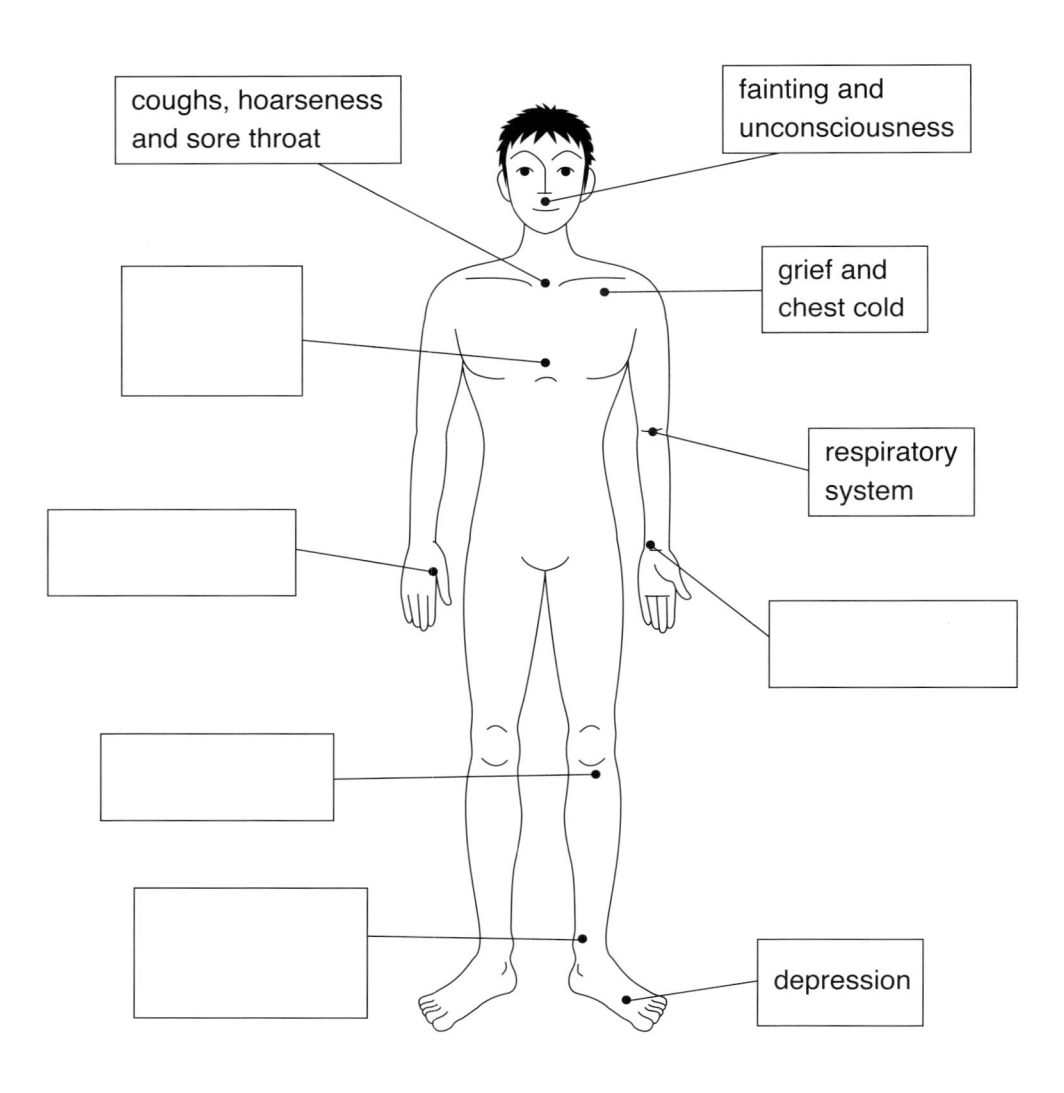

- coughs, hoarseness and sore throat
- fainting and unconsciousness
- grief and chest cold
- respiratory system
- depression

Unit 11

Acupuncture — On Pins and Needles

MODEL DIALOGUE — JIGSAW LISTENING

Student A (Student B, see page 113)

Listen, repeat and fill in the blanks.

A: Hi, Ian. What are you _____ to your _____ with that _____?

B: Hi, Jackie. Can't you tell I'm administering "shiatsu" therapy?

A: "Shiatsu"? What _____ that _____? Is that some kind of _____ medicine?

B: Yes, it's a kind of therapy. Pressure is put on acupuncture points, usually with the fingers, but sometimes with a special pen.

A: So, you _____, it's like acupuncture but uses fingers _____ of _____?

B: Exactly. I'm now using my pen instead of my finger.

A: Where's the point for a _____ neck? I always have _____ in my neck and _____, too.

B: Oh, you do? Let me try my healing pen on your shoulder. Come on.

A: Well, actually, I'm already _____ and have to go. Thanks, _____.

B: All right. Next time we meet, I'll show you some pressure points for sore muscles.

A: I'm _____ I'll still have some _____ _____ then!

ACT OUT THE DIALOGUE

Work with your partner.
1. Silently and quickly read and remember one line at a time.
2. Look up at your partner and speak while keeping eye contact.
3. Change roles and practice again by replacing some parts with your own words.

77

FACT DICTATION

Here are some interesting facts. Listen and fill in the blanks.

1. Many experts _____ acupuncture _____ _____ safer than many well-established _____.

2. More than one million Americans _____ acupuncture therapy to treat _____ _____ of _____.

3. Commonly _____ ailments _____ _____ headaches to arthritis and _____.

4. Acupuncture is often recommended _____ _____ problems like lower _____ _____ and _____.

5. Nausea, _____ _____ of pregnancy and cancer chemotherapy, can also be _____.

6. Unfortunately, many _____ providers _____ to _____ the _____ of acupuncture treatments.

7. Further _____ is _____ to _____ the benefits and _____ of acupuncture.

IN YOUR OWN WORDS

a. Name three symptoms that acupuncture may effectively treat.
-
-
-

b. Name three symptoms that acupuncture may not be able to treat.
-
-
-

CRITICAL THINKING — Begging the question

Explain what is wrong with the following statement:
> Why doesn't acupuncture work? Because it is not Western-style medicine, it originated from Chinese medicine.

Unit 12

Three Major Causes of Death—Are You Insured?

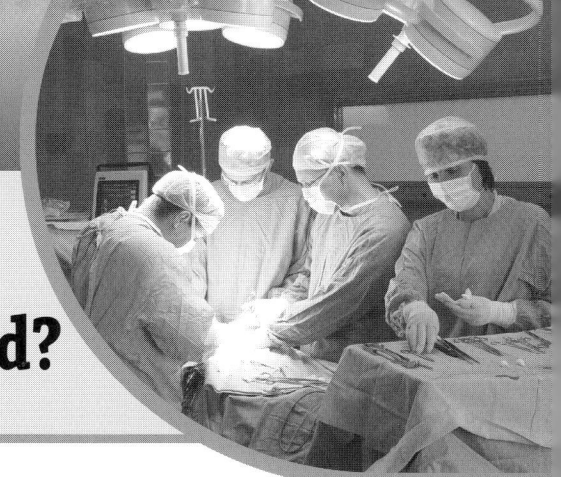

MATCHING

Match the words (1-9) with the correct definitions (a-i).

1. ___ cause
2. ___ disease
3. ___ blood vessels
4. ___ hemorrhage
5. ___ acute
6. ___ plaque
7. ___ stroke
8. ___ develop
9. ___ abnormal

a. unusual or atypical in a way that seems strange or wrong
b. very strong; serious, sharp
c. a person, event, or thing that makes something happen
d. to grow or change into something bigger, stronger, or more advanced
e. a type of illness which is caused by bacteria or an infection
f. serious bleeding, sometimes inside the body
g. a fat deposit on the inside wall of an artery
h. a sudden burst or blockage of an artery (tube carrying blood) in the brain
i. tubes through which blood flows in your body

GAP-FILL EXERCISE

Complete the sentences with the words from MATCHING.

1. _____ in the arteries can cause disease.
2. His friends were worried about his _____ behavior.
3. After the operation, the patient was in _____ pain.
4. _____ is the medical term for internal bleeding.
5. The _____ of the accident is unknown.
6. Arteries, capillaries and veins are _____.
7. Don't wait for a problem to _____ before having a health check.
8. Many _____s can be controlled by antibacterial drugs.
9. The elderly woman died of a sudden _____.

VOCABULARY ANALOGIES

Analogies show how words are related. For example, LISTEN is to SOUND as SEE is to SIGHT.

1. **Insurance** is to **coverage** as **policies** is to _____.
   a. plans   b. deaths   c. statistics
2. **Abnormal** is to **normal** as **insufficient** is to _____.
   a. lack   b. shortage   c. sufficient
3. **Internal** is to **inner** as **supply** is to _____.
   a. demand   b. give   c. oxygen
4. **Paralysis** is to **loss** as **radiation** is to _____.
   a. ability   b. move   c. energy
5. **Circulation** is to **flow** as **blockage** is to _____.
   a. blood   b. clot   c. storage
6. **Cerebral** is to **brain** as **hemorrhagic** is to _____.
   a. internal   b. bleeding   c. stomach
7. **Acute** is to **sharp** as **chronic** is to _____.
   a. long-term   b. short-term   c. temporary

BEFORE YOU LISTEN

Listen for answers to the following questions.
1. What are three major diseases leading to death in Japan?
2. What can strokes cause?
3. How does a heart attack happen?

LISTEN

Close the textbook and take notes about the key information.

Do you know what the three major causes of death in Japan are? They are cancer, stroke and heart attacks. Since the diseases that cause these deaths are all very serious, many life insurance *(5)* companies recommend including coverage for them on their policies.

Cancer is a disease in which abnormal cells grow out of control and they can spread all over the body. If *(10)* these bad cells develop in the stomach, it becomes stomach cancer. If they develop

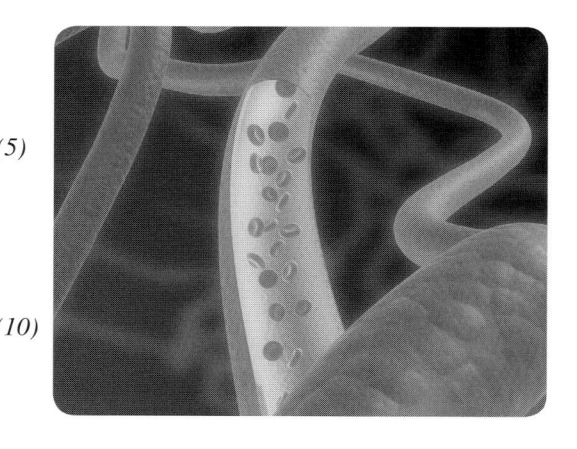

Unit 12
Three Major Causes of Death — Are You Insured?

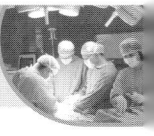

in a lung, it becomes lung cancer. If this happens with blood cells and the white blood cell count increases excessively, it is called leukemia. In this way, cancer can be the cause of many kinds of diseases. There are three common treatments for cancer: radiation therapy, operation and drug therapy. *(15)*

A stroke happens when something goes wrong with the blood circulation in the brain. It can cause paralysis of the body. There are two main types of strokes — hemorrhagic and ischemic. Hemorrhages or internal bleeding cause hemorrhagic strokes. A lack of blood supply or decreased blood flow in the brain causes ischemic strokes. *(20)* According to statistics, only one of six strokes is from internal bleeding and the rest are from insufficient blood flow. Cerebral strokes, as doctors properly call both kinds of strokes, are the third most common cause of death, and one of the main causes of disability in Japan.

A heart attack, more commonly called a myocardial infarction or acute myocardial *(25)* infarction in hospitals, occurs when the blood supply to the heart is blocked. Without blood flow, oxygen cannot get to the heart muscle, and without oxygen the heart muscle becomes damaged and starts to die. So what inside the body blocks this blood flow? It is a kind of fat called plaque that builds up on the inner walls of the arteries that supply blood and oxygen to your heart. Eventually, the plaque falls away from the blood vessel *(30)* wall and blocks the vessel, which causes a blood clot to form. If the clot becomes larger, it can completely block the flow of blood.

CHECK YOUR COMPREHENSION

a. Answer the following questions.
   1. What are the three major causes of death in Japan?
   2. What is cancer?
   3. What are strokes a main cause of?
   4. What are heart attacks called in hospitals?
   5. What does plaque do to your arteries?

b. Correct the following statements.
   1. Leukemia is a disease in which the red blood cell count increases dramatically.
   2. Radiation therapy and drug therapy are the only treatments for cancer.
   3. There are three main types of strokes.
   4. Internal bleeding causes most strokes.
   5. A heart attack causes too much oxygen to flow to heart muscle.

QUESTIONS AND ANSWERS — Body Organs

Student A (Student B, see page 114)

a. Memorize and ask these questions to Student B and complete your chart.
1. Where is the (stomach) located?
2. Could you draw the shape of the (stomach)?
3. What is a function of the (stomach)?
4. What is a possible illness of the (stomach)?

Name of Organ	Location	Shape	Function	Possible Illness
stomach			to digest food	
	in the abdomen	(shape)		liver cancer
spleen			to control the quality of blood	
	between the stomach and anus	(shape)		tumor
kidneys			to send waste matter as urine	
	behind the stomach	(shape)		diabetes

b. Answer the following questions.
1. Which organ can work even if reduced to one quarter of its original size and is called "a silent organ"?
2. Which organ is the appendix attached to?
3. Which organ was believed to cause temper tantrums?

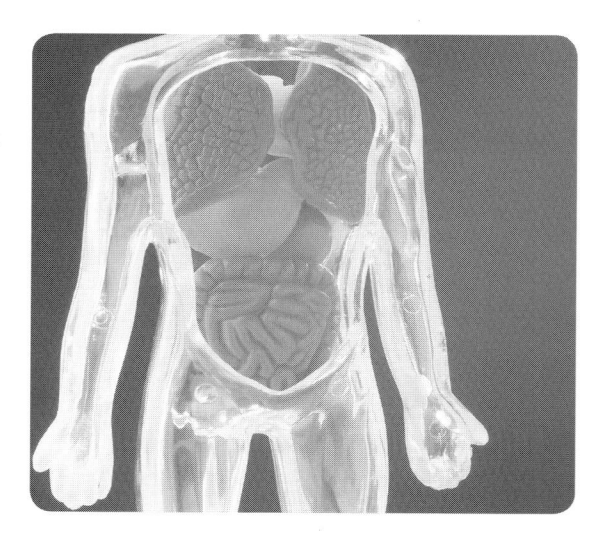

Unit 12
Three Major Causes of Death — Are You Insured?

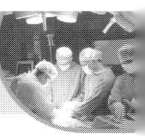

MODEL DIALOGUE — JIGSAW LISTENING

Student A (Student B, see page 115)

Listen, repeat and fill in the blanks.

A: Hi, Bill.
B: George, what's wrong? You don't look so good.
A: I just had a _____ _____ in the _____ of my chest.
B: When did you have that? How long did it last?
A: Just now. I had _____ pain and felt sick _____ my _____. It _____ like forever.
B: Do you have other pains?
A: That was _____. I felt so bad _____ my chest, I didn't _____ much _____.
B: Did you feel like vomiting or break out in a cold sweat?
A: Yes, I _____, actually. How did you know? My _____ _____ body felt _____, too.
B: Here, put this aspirin under your tongue. It reduces blood clotting. You better have that checked out right away.
A: Thank you. I'll go to the _____ right _____. I'll _____ _____ my car.
B: Don't go by car. Let me call 9-1-1 for an ambulance.
A: Is it _____ _____?
B: It's better to be safe.

ACT OUT THE DIALOGUE

Work with your partner.
1. Silently and quickly read and remember one line at a time.
2. Look up at your partner and speak while keeping eye contact.
3. Change roles and practice again by replacing some parts with your own words.

83

FACT DICTATION

Here are some facts regarding a matter of life and death. Listen and fill in the blanks.

1. Stroke _____ _____ _____ deadly _____ many people can survive _____ strokes.
2. To _____ yourself _____ strokes, you have to know _____ the _____ are.
3. Your hand, _____ right hand, may _____ like "pins and _____."
4. You cannot speak _____ because your _____ _____ _____ and heavy.
5. You _____ when you walk and _____ someone to _____ you.
6. Although _____ symptoms may _____ away, _____ medical help immediately.
7. By _____ the _____ symptoms, you may _____ someone's _____, maybe your _____.

IN YOUR OWN WORDS

a. List three things that cause hypertension (high blood pressure).
-
-
-

b. Name three things that lower blood pressure.
-
-
-

CRITICAL THINKING — Oversimplification of cause

Explain what is wrong with the following statement:
   Many people get cancer because they drink or smoke. As for me, I don't drink or smoke and I am a vegetarian, so I will not get cancer.

Review Unit 7-12

TOEHM
(Test of English for Health Matters)

Part 1   **Picture Descriptions (Vocabulary Review)**

You will hear three short statements. Look at the picture and choose the statement that best describes what you see in the picture.

1.

A   B   C

2.

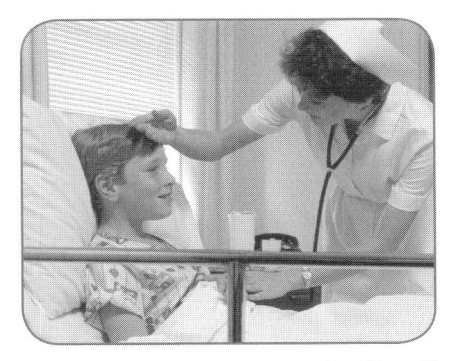

A   B   C

3.

A   B   C

4.

A   B   C

Part 2 Question - Response

You will hear a question followed by three responses. You are to choose the best response to each question.

1. Mark your answer.　　A　B　C
2. Mark your answer.　　A　B　C
3. Mark your answer.　　A　B　C
4. Mark your answer.　　A　B　C
5. Mark your answer.　　A　B　C
6. Mark your answer.　　A　B　C

Part 3 Short Conversations

You will hear short conversations between two people. You will read three questions about each conversation followed by three answers. You are to choose the best answer to each question.

1. What is the man's problem?
   A. He is a pain in the neck.
   B. He has neck and shoulder pain.
   C. He used to be nervous.

2. What would the man like to do?
   A. Undergo acupuncture therapy
   B. Become more honest
   C. Take away his nervousness

3. What most likely is the woman's occupation?
   A. A dentist
   B. A psychologist
   C. An acupuncturist

4. Who most likely are the speakers?
   A. Doctor and patient
   B. Parent and nutritionist
   C. Colleagues

5. What are the speakers talking about?
   A. A barometer
   B. A device
   C. Footsteps

6. For what is a pedometer used?
   A. Holding medicine
   B. Taking walks
   C. Counting steps

Review Unit 7-12

TOEHM (Test of English for Health Matters)

Part 4 Short Talk

You will hear a short talk (announcement, advertisement, report, speech, etc.). You will read three questions about the talk followed by three answers. Select the best answer to each question.

1. Who is speaking?
   A. A doctor
   B. A radio broadcaster
   C. A school counselor

2. What is the talk about?
   A. Chest symptoms
   B. Nausea and light-headedness
   C. Myocardial infarctions

3. What is NOT a sign of a heart attack?
   A. Shortness of breath
   B. Discomfort in the legs
   C. Nausea

Part 5 Incomplete Sentences

A word or phrase is missing in each of the sentences below. Select the best answer to complete the sentence.

1. They _____ a nine-year study observing more than 3,000 people.
   A. comprised
   B. conducted
   C. connected

2. The term "Type A personality" became a _____ in the United States.
   A. codeword
   B. catchword
   C. buzzword

3. Bread made from refined grains has _____ textures and longer shelf lives than whole grains.
   A. fine
   B. finer
   C. finest

4. When you smell coffee, you _____ help waking up.
   A. can
   B. cannot
   C. must

5. _____ people are people who do little or no exercise.
   A. Energetic
   B. Sedentary
   C. Vigorous

6. Regular exercise can slow down the _____ of muscle mass.
   A. deterioration
   B. improvement
   C. recuperation

7. The energy in the acupuncture channels can be _____ with metal needles.
   A. regulate
   B. regulated
   C. regulation

8. Cancer is a disease in which _____ cells grow out of control.
   A. average
   B. normal
   C. abnormal

9. The pediatrician was sometimes too direct and _____ to be effective with children.
   A. thoughtful
   B. blunt
   C. keen

10. Evidently, his emotion was _____ by aromatherapy.
    A. affected
    B. effected
    C. perfected

11. This consent form authorizes the nurses to _____ prescription medicine, at your request.
    A. consist
    B. undergo
    C. administer

12. His heart rate increased rapidly and he _____ out in a cold sweat.
    A. broke
    B. honked
    C. stated

Part 6 Reading Comprehension : Chart

Read the text (article, letter, advertisement, webpage) followed by four questions. Select the best answer to each question.

DIETARY FATS COMPARISON

OILS NAMES	Saturated Fat	Monosaturated Fat	Polyunsaturated Fats - Linolenic (Omega-6)	Polyunsaturated Fats - Alpha-Linolenic (Omega-3)
Canola Oil	7	63	20	10
Flax Oil	9	19	17	55
Safflower Oil	9	14	77	0
Grape Seed Oil	10	22	68	0
Sunflower Oil	11	23	66	0
Corn Oil	14	32	52	2
Olive Oil	14	76	10	0
Soybean Oil	15	23	54	8
Peanut Oil	19	45	34	2
Cottonseed Oil	26	16	58	0
Palm Oil	51	39	10	0

(Content Percentage)

1. Which oil contains the highest percentage of saturated fat?
   A. Olive oil
   B. Grape seed oil
   C. Palm oil

2. Which of these oils does not contain Omega-3?
   A. Canola oil
   B. Cottonseed oil
   C. Peanut oil

3. Which oil contains the highest percentage of polyunsaturated fat?
   A. Flax oil
   B. Safflower oil
   C. Corn oil

4. Which oil contains the most monosaturated fat?
   A. Olive oil
   B. Peanut oil
   C. Soybean oil

Part 7 Reading Comprehension : Text

Read the text (article, letter, advertisement, webpage) followed by four questions. Select the best answer to each question.

SALT & SODIUM

What is sodium? Sodium is a mineral element that is commonly found in salt. It also occurs naturally in much smaller amounts in animal and plant foods and even in water. In fact, we normally consume enough salt for our dietary needs without needing to add salt.

Our bodies require sodium in order for our nerves and muscles to function properly and to balance the amount of fluid in our tissues and blood. Sodium is like a sponge that attracts and holds fluids in body tissues. Too much sodium can cause water retention and increase the risk of hypertension, commonly known as high blood pressure. Too little sodium may cause hypotension or low blood pressure, and decrease blood flow to the heart, brain and kidneys.

1. Where is this article likely to be found?
   A. An encyclopedia
   B. A health magazine
   C. A medical journal

2. What does sodium NOT do?
   A. Make fluids in body tissues
   B. Hold fluids in body tissues
   C. Attract fluids in body tissues

3. What is hypotension also known as?
   A. Low blood pressure
   B. Normal blood pressure
   C. High blood pressure

4. What does the report NOT suggest about sodium?
   A. The lack of it reduces blood flow to the heart, stomach and kidneys.
   B. We take in enough of it through our daily diets.
   C. It causes the amount of fluid in our bodies to be out of balance.

Student B Pages

- Questions and Answers
- Model Dialogue — Jigsaw Listening

Unit 1 Why English? The Basis for Academic Inquiry

QUESTIONS AND ANSWERS

a. Memorize and ask these questions to Student A and complete your chart.
1. What is (Alfred)'s first language?
2. What is (Alfred)'s occupation?
3. Where does (Alfred) work?
4. What English journal does (Alfred) read?

Name	First Language	Occupation	Department / Workplace	Name of Journal
Alfred	Chinese		internal medicine	
Benjamin		surgeon		Journal of Clinical Investigation
Charlie	Tagalog		dentistry	
David		pharmacist		Science
Edward	Russian		pediatrics	
Frank		resident		Journal of Experimental Medicine

b. Answer the following questions.
1. Who should you go to if you are pregnant?
2. Who would you go to if your child got sick?
3. What language do you use when reading websites?

Unit 1
Student B

MODEL DIALOGUE — JIGSAW LISTENING

Listen, repeat and fill in the blanks.

A: Hi, Judy, how's your first year in college going?
B: Hi, Ed, I'm _____ so much. I feel like a _____ again!
A: That's great to feel like that. I'm just the opposite. My classes are rather boring, and nothing relates to my major.
B: So, that's why it's good to take _____ classes, _____ it? You need to learn things _____ your _____. That makes you more _____.
A: I'm really only interested in my major.
B: Oh, come on! _____ _____ _____ you don't care about the big questions in life, _____ we are, _____ we are going, or _____ the world works?
A: My major is medicine, so I'll mainly be studying that for the rest of my life. Why should I waste time with all those other things?
B: Of course, you are _____ in medicine, _____ you study English, too. What _____ that?
A: I study English because I have to. It's required. I wouldn't bother otherwise. How about yourself?
B: I'm _____ a foreign language because it _____ me different _____ of _____. It _____ my _____ up and _____ my brain _____ in new ways.
A: Uh, I've never thought about it like that. I only use Japanese to think.
B: Then your _____ to think is _____ to just one way. That's too _____, don't you _____?

ACT OUT THE DIALOGUE

Work with your partner.
1. Silently and quickly read and remember one line at a time.
2. Look up at your partner and speak while keeping eye contact.
3. Change roles and practice again by replacing some parts with your own words.

93

Unit 2 Sleep — Sweet Dreams

QUESTIONS AND ANSWERS

a. Memorize and ask these questions to Student A and complete your chart.
   1. Is (Alfred) ever late for class?
   2. What time does (Alfred) usually go to sleep?
   3. What does (Alfred) do before going to bed?
   4. How long does (Alfred) sleep every day?

Name	Late for Class	Bed Time	Before Bed	Sleeping Hours
Alfred	always		plays computer games	
Benjamin		midnight		four hours and a half
Charlie	sometimes		does some stretches	
David		ten o'clock at night		seven and a half hours
You				
Partner				

b. Answer the following questions.
   1. Who gets up earliest?
   2. Who sleeps the longest?
   3. Who has the healthiest sleeping habits?

Unit 2
Student B

MODEL DIALOGUE — JIGSAW LISTENING

Listen, repeat and fill in the blanks.

A: Hi, John, how are you doing?
B: Oh, hi, Sara, I'm a _____ _____ today. I felt _____ all day yesterday.
A: What seems to be the problem?
B: I haven't _____ much sleep _____. I think I might have _____.
A: What time do you usually go to bed?
B: _____ 12 o'clock, after _____ TV and _____ _____.
A: I've heard TV and alcohol just make insomnia worse.
B: Maybe. It seems _____ _____ these days. How _____ you? What _____ you usually do _____ going to bed?
A: I usually do some stretching and drink a glass of warm milk.
B: Does _____ _____?
A: Almost always, yes.
B: So, you never have _____ _____ _____ _____?
A: Not really. I've never used sleeping pills, either. Just a good stretch and some milk.
B: I never take pills, _____, but I definitely need a _____ sleep _____.

ACT OUT THE DIALOGUE

Work with your partner.
1. Silently and quickly read and remember one line at a time.
2. Look up at your partner and speak while keeping eye contact.
3. Change roles and practice again by replacing some parts with information about yourself.

Unit 3 Allergies — Got an Itch to Scratch?

QUESTIONS AND ANSWERS

a. Memorize and ask these questions to Student A and complete your chart.
1. What seems to be (Edward)'s problem?
2. What can be a cause of allergy to (Edward)?
3. What does (Edward) do to prevent the allergy?
4. What (medicine) does (Edward) take to cure the symptom?

Name	Problem / Symptom	Causes of the Allergy	Ways to Prevent	Medicine
Edward	itchy eyes		putting on goggles	
Frank		Japanese cypress		antihistamine medicine
George	skin rash; hives		avoiding seafood	
Harry		monosodium glutamate (MSG)		antiallergy drug
You				
Partner				

b. Answer the following questions.
1. Whose allergy seems to be the most severe? Why?
2. What are other ways to cure allergies?
3. Whose allergy seems to be the most curable? Why?

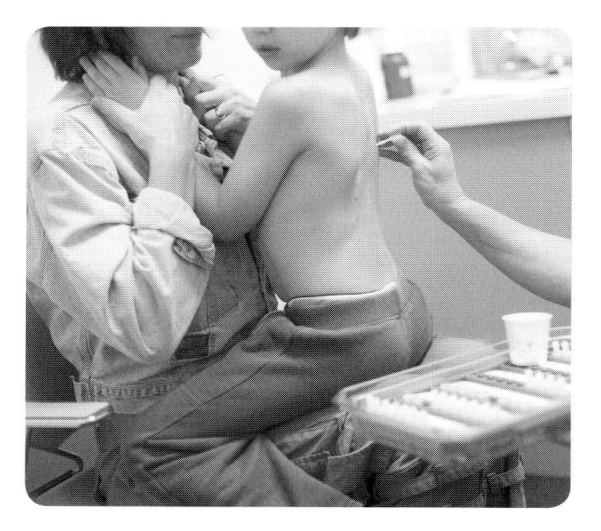

Unit 3
Student B

MODEL DIALOGUE — JIGSAW LISTENING

Listen, repeat and fill in the blanks.

A: Hello, Mr. Takeda. What seems to be the problem today?
B: Hello, doctor. I have a _____ nose, no matter _____ much I _____ my nose.
A: I can hear your nose is stuffed up, with a bit of a scratch to your voice, too. Does your throat feel itchy?
B: Yes, and my eyes are _____, too. Really, it _____ everywhere.
A: What color is your mucus? Is it yellow or colorless like water?
B: Like _____. My eyes are _____ all the _____, too.
A: When did all this start? Any particular time?
B: It started _____ after I _____ to a new apartment.
A: Did you notice anything unusual in the new place?
B. It's a _____ old and very _____, but there's nothing _____ about it.
A: Does this happen all the time, like every year during the spring or …?
B: No, it _____ never _____ to me before.
A: Well, then. You might have an allergy to house dust.
B: What does that _____? Is there _____ I can do _____ it? Do I have to move again?

ACT OUT THE DIALOGUE

Work with your partner.
1. Silently and quickly read and remember one line at a time.
2. Look up at your partner and speak while keeping eye contact.
3. Change roles and practice again by replacing some parts with your own words.

Unit 4 Stress Management — Don't Let It Get to You!

QUESTIONS AND ANSWERS

a. Memorize and ask these questions to Student A and complete your chart.
   1. What seems to be (Edward)'s problem?
   2. What can be a cause of stress to (Edward)?
   3. What does (Edward) do to relax?
   4. What kind of person is (Edward)?

Name	Problem / Symptom	Cause of Stress	Way to Relax	Personality
Edward	ulcers		exercises	
Frank		relationships at work		moody
George	teeth grinding / gnashing		meditates	
Harry		ailment: rheumatism		naïve
You				
Partner				

b. Answer the following questions.
   1. Who seems to be under a great deal of stress? Why?
   2. Who has the best stress management strategy?

Unit 4
Student B

MODEL DIALOGUE — JIGSAW LISTENING

Listen, repeat and fill in the blanks.

A: Hey there. How are you today?
B: Oh, hi, Jane, I'm _____ not _____ today.
A: What's the matter?
B: I'm _____ with schoolwork.
A: You do seem a little stressed out.
B: I have too _____ to do and too _____ _____.
A: If you need some help, I'm right here. Just let me know what I can do.
B: Thanks. It's _____ something I have to _____ _____ myself. Thank you for _____, _____.
A: The best thing is to take it easy. Do one thing at a time by making a plan.
B: Yeah, I _____, but I'm _____ _____ busy to _____ make plans.
A: That sounds familiar. I've been in that situation before.
B: So, how did you _____ your stress _____?

ACT OUT THE DIALOGUE

Work with your partner.
1. Silently and quickly read and remember one line at a time.
2. Look up at your partner and speak while keeping eye contact.
3. Change roles and practice again by replacing some parts with your own words.

99

Unit 5 Skin — Beauty is Only Skin Deep

QUESTIONS AND ANSWERS

a. Memorize and ask these questions to Student A and complete your chart.
1. What seems to be (Edward)'s problem?
2. Since when has (Edward) had this?
3. What does (Edward) do to prevent the problem?
4. What (medicine) does (Edward) take to treat the symptom?

Name	Problem / Symptom	How did it happen?	Cause(s)	Treatment(s)
Edward		ate unusual fish		ointment / salve
Frank	itchy toes		athlete's foot; fungus infection	
George		has been eating high-fat foods		acne creams and vitamin B pills
Harry	blisters		burns	
You				
Partner				

b. Answer the following questions.
1. Whose skin condition can be infectious/ contagious/ transmitted?
2. Whose condition may take the longest to cure? Why?

Unit 5
Student B

MODEL DIALOGUE — JIGSAW LISTENING

Listen, repeat and fill in the blanks.

A: Hello, Henry. Long time no see. How have you been?
B: Yes, it's been _____ _____, Melinda. I've been OK. You _____ changed a _____.
A: Thank you, I've been working out lately. What about you? Your skin looks a little red.
B: Well, I was _____ in the _____ too long, _____ golf.
A: Is it painful when your skin peels off?
B: Yes, it really _____. I _____ SPF _____ _____, but maybe too _____.
A: That helps. It blocks UV-A. I wear sunscreen all year round.
B: No _____ you don't look _____ _____ older than when we first _____.
A: Thanks. I try to take good care of myself.
B: So, what's _____ _____ to being so healthy? Just the _____?
A: There are a few other secrets, too!
B: Do _____!

ACT OUT THE DIALOGUE

Work with your partner.
1. Silently and quickly read and remember one line at a time.
2. Look up at your partner and speak while keeping eye contact.
3. Change roles and practice again by replacing some parts with your own words.

Unit 6 Sports Injuries — RICE is Nice

QUESTIONS AND ANSWERS

a. Memorize and ask these questions to Student A and complete your chart.

1. How did (Fumie) (sprain) her (finger)?
2. What happened to (Fumie) yesterday?
3. When did (Fumie) (sprain) her (finger)?

- She was (playing) (ping-pong).
- She (sprained) her (finger).
- It happened (yesterday).

sprained wrist
How? ....
When? ....

What? *sprained finger*
How? *playing ping-pong*
When? *yesterday*

broken nose
How? ....
this morning

What? ....
playing soccer
yesterday afternoon

What? ....
skateboarding
When? ....

What? ....
playing basketball
last week

b. Answer the following questions.

1. Who has the most severe injury?
2. Whose injury is the most recent?
3. What sport may cause injuries most often?

Unit 6

Student B

MODEL DIALOGUE — JIGSAW LISTENING

Listen, repeat and fill in the blanks.

A: Hi, John. Have you seen Jim recently? I haven't seen him around for a while.

B: Yes, as a _____ of fact. I saw him _____ day, walking _____ crutches and _____ a _____.

A: A sling and crutches? What happened?

B: He _____ himself playing football _____ weekend.

A: You mean soccer or rugby?

B: American _____, _____.

A: How did that happen?

B: He said he _____ in the middle of the _____ and three other guys fell right _____ him.

A: Ouch! That sounds very painful. Where was he taken, St. Luke's Hospital?

B: Yes, and he got _____ on his _____, too. Hey, speak of the _____, here he _____ right now.

A: Hey, there's the football star! Who won the game, Jim? No, seriously, are you all right?

ACT OUT THE DIALOGUE

Work with your partner.
1. Silently and quickly read and remember one line at a time.
2. Look up at your partner and speak while keeping eye contact.
3. Change roles and practice again by replacing some parts with your own words.

Scoring Guide for the Behavior Test in Unit 7

1. (a) 15 points, (b) 5 points, (c) 2 points
2. (a) 20 points, (b) 10 points, (c) 5 points
3. (a) 25 points, (b) 15 points, (c) 5 points, (d) 0 point
4. (a) 15 points, (b) 5 points, (c) 2 points
5. (a) 20 points, (b) 10 points, (c) 2 points
6. (a) 50 points, (b) 30 points, (c) 2 points
7. (a) 2 points, (b) 2 points, (c) 5 points, (d) 15 points
8. (a) 50 points, (b) 30 points, (c) 2 points
9. (a) 70 points, (b) 50 points, (c) 10 points, (d) 5 points
10. (a) 2 points, (b) 5 points, (c) 10 points, (d) 15 points
11. (a) 3 points, (b) 10 points, (c) 20 points
12. (a) 20 points, (b) 15 points, (c) 10 points, (d) 3 points

Unit 7 Personality — You Need to Chill Out!

QUESTIONS AND ANSWERS

Partner B asks the even-numbered questions. Check your partner's answers in the boxes ☐ and your answers in the circles ○.

1. _____?
   - ☐ Faster than most people ○ a
   - ☐ Average speed ○ b
   - ☐ Slower than most people ○ c

2. When you have a problem, what do you usually do?
   - ☐ Take action immediately ○ a
   - ☐ Think and then take action ○ b
   - ☐ Wait for the problem to fix itself ○ c

3. _____?
   - ☐ Before all of your classmates ○ a
   - ☐ Before most of your classmates ○ b
   - ☐ Just on time ○ c
   - ☐ Late ○ d

4. How quickly do you usually eat?
   - ☐ Faster than most people ○ a
   - ☐ Average speed ○ b
   - ☐ Slower than most people ○ c

5. _____?
   - ☐ Often ○ a
   - ☐ Sometimes ○ b
   - ☐ Almost never ○ c

6. When you play games, how important is it to win?
   - ☐ Very important ○ a
   - ☐ Sometimes important ○ b
   - ☐ Not important ○ c

7. _____?
   - ☐ Almost always ○ a
   - ☐ Sometimes ○ b
   - ☐ Almost never ○ c
   - ☐ Never ○ d

8. At school, how important is it to be the best student?
   - ☐ Very important ○ a
   - ☐ Sometimes important ○ b
   - ☐ Not important ○ c

9. _____?
   - ☐ Always hardworking and serious ○ a
   - ☐ Sometimes hardworking and serious ○ b
   - ☐ Rarely hardworking and serious ○ c
   - ☐ Lazy and not serious ○ d

10. What do you like to do in your free time?
    - ☐ Sleep ○ a
    - ☐ Watch TV ○ b
    - ☐ Go shopping ○ c
    - ☐ Clean your room ○ d

11. _____?
    - ☐ Never ○ a
    - ☐ Sometimes ○ b
    - ☐ Always ○ c

12. When do you begin to study for an important test?
    - ☐ Two weeks ahead ○ a
    - ☐ One week ahead ○ b
    - ☐ A day before ○ c
    - ☐ Don't study! ○ d

The scoring guide is on page 103
If your score is less than 150, you have a Type B personality.
If your score is more than 150, you have a Type A personality.

Unit 7
Student B

MODEL DIALOGUE — JIGSAW LISTENING

Listen, repeat and fill in the blanks.

A: Hey, Mike, what are you doing?
B: Oh, hi, Sue. I'm _____ a personality _____.
A: A personality test? You've got to be kidding! What if you fail and have no personality?
B: Very _____. Everyone has a personality. Actually, this _____ test is quite _____.
A: What's so special about it?
B: Well, this test can _____ _____ I am a Type A or Type B person.
A: Aha! You don't need a test. I can tell you already. You are a typical Type A person.
B: I _____?
A: Yes, you are impatient and too detail-oriented.
B: Ouch! You _____ me too _____. Thanks for being _____ honest!
A: Sorry to be so blunt. I'm too direct sometimes. Maybe I'm a little Type A, too!
B: That's okay. I'm trying to _____ _____ of a Type B person. I've started _____ to help me relax.
A: That's a good start. Why don't you try listening to classical music, too?
B: Thanks. I'll give _____ a _____. In a few weeks, I'll _____ a new person.

ACT OUT THE DIALOGUE

Work with your partner.
1. Silently and quickly read and remember one line at a time.
2. Look up at your partner and speak while keeping eye contact.
3. Change roles and practice again by replacing some parts with your own words.

105

Unit 8 Nutrition — Nutritious is Delicious

QUESTIONS AND ANSWERS

a. Memorize and ask these questions to Student A and complete your chart.
1. What country is number (1)?
2. How many grams are recommended in (Canada)?
3. How many servings are recommended in (Canada)?

Ranking	Country	Number of Grams	Recommended Servings
1	Japan		4 portions of fruits and 13 portions of vegetables
2		800	
3	India		4 portions of fruits and 5 portions of vegetables
4		720	
5	Slovenia		13 portions of fruits and vegetables
6		625	
7	Ukraine		6 portions of fruits and vegetables
8		600	
9	Australia		2 portions of fruits and 5 portions of vegetables
10		400	

b. Answer the following questions.
1. Which country recommends the most vegetables?
2. Which country uses the largest serving size?
3. Which country recommends the least fruits?

Unit 8
Student B

MODEL DIALOGUE — JIGSAW LISTENING

Listen, repeat and fill in the blanks.

A: Lisa, what's up?
B: Not _____, David. I'm just _____ at this _____ guidebook.
A: Nutrition? Where did this sudden interest come from?
B: I _____ a documentary about _____ last night and I _____ to learn more.
A: What did you find out?
B: Well, I _____ that I've been _____ too many high-fat foods, _____ like doughnuts.
A: Me, too. I'm sure it's high in fat, but those things taste so good.
B: That's just the _____.
A: What does the book say we should be eating instead?
B: Well, we should _____ more _____ and _____, of course.
A: That's easy! I'm crazy about mangosteens and lychees.
B: You are. Really? Those are a little _____ to _____ sometimes. I'm not a big _____ of lychees _____.
A: How can you not like lychees?
B: Lychees are _____ to eat. I prefer more _____ fruits like apples and bananas.
A: To each his own, I suppose.

ACT OUT THE DIALOGUE

Work with your partner.
1. Silently and quickly read and remember one line at a time.
2. Look up at your partner and speak while keeping eye contact.
3. Change roles and practice again by replacing some parts with your own words.

107

Unit 9 Aromatherapy — What's that Smell?

QUESTIONS AND ANSWERS

a. Memorize and ask these questions to Student A and complete your chart.
1. How is (basil) oil used?
2. What can be used as (an antidepressant)?
3. What can be used to (relieve stress)?

Essential Oil	Uses	
basil oil	•	• to relieve headaches
black pepper oil	• to stimulate circulation	•
citronella oil	•	
clove oil	• as a topical analgesic	•
eucalyptus oil	•	• to soothe minor cuts and burns
geranium oil	• as a diuretic	•
lavender oil	• to help breathing in case of cold	
lemon oil	•	• as an antidepressant
rose oil	• as an aphrodisiac	
tea tree oil	•	• as a disinfectant

b. Answer the following questions.
1. Which essential oils can be used as antiseptics?
2. Which essential oil has the most uses?
3. Which essential oil can be used as a disinfectant?

Unit 9

Student B

MODEL DIALOGUE — JIGSAW LISTENING

Listen, repeat and fill in the blanks.

A: Ben, do you smell something?
B: Is it _____, Kate? I _____ not.
A: No, I don't think it's you, but what is that smell?
B: Maybe it's the _____ freshener I _____ a few minutes _____.
A: No, I don't think it's the air freshener. That would smell good!
B: (*Sniff, Sniff*) Yeah, you're right. Something _____. It's kind of _____ even.
A: Have you been cooking something with, say garlic?
B: No. I haven't _____ for weeks, I'm embarrassed _____ _____.
A: How can you live without cooking?
B: Oh, don't get me _____. I eat, but I just don't _____.
A: When was the last time you ate a good, solid, home-cooked meal?
B: Well, last _____, I had oregano-_____ lamb shank with a delicious _____.
A: Well, it sounds like you are a gourmet.
B: Not _____, but I do like good food. I just never _____ time to _____ it!
A: Well, invite me next time you do!

ACT OUT THE DIALOGUE

Work with your partner.
1. Silently and quickly read and remember one line at a time.
2. Look up at your partner and speak while keeping eye contact.
3. Change roles and practice again by replacing some parts with your own words.

109

Unit 10 Aging — Forever Young

QUESTIONS AND ANSWERS

a. Memorize and ask these questions to Student A and complete your chart.
1. What is (Alfred)'s height and weight?
2. What is the percentage of (Alfred)'s body fat?
3. What exercise does (Alfred) do?
4. What is (Alfred)'s pulse rate?

Name	Height & Weight	Body Fat Percentage	Exercise	Pulse Rate
Alfred		16%		63 beats per minute
Benjamin	165 cm 58 kg		jogging	
Charlie		9%		72 beats per minute
David	167 cm 80 kg		bowling	
Ellie		18%		81 beats per minute
Partner				

b. Answer the following questions.
1. Which exercise burns the least energy?
2. Who seems to be the healthiest? Why?
3. Ten years from now, what will your partner's pulse rate be?

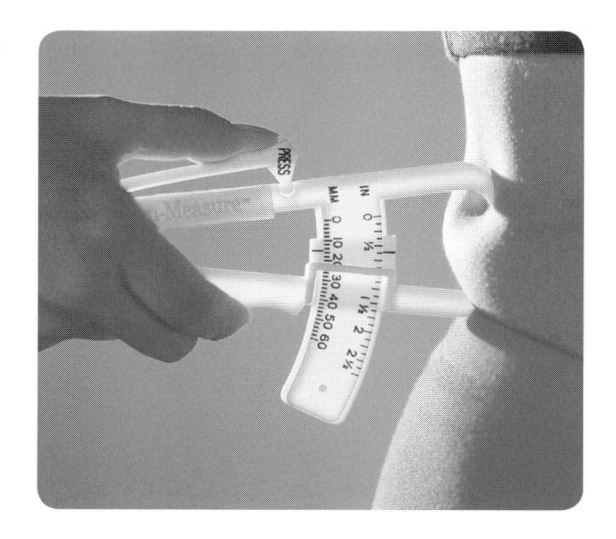

Unit 10

Student B

MODEL DIALOGUE — JIGSAW LISTENING

Listen, repeat and fill in the blanks.

A: Rachel, this may sound like a strange question, but have you ever thought about your future?
B: No, not _____. I'm _____ on the _____ and now.
A: Well then, can you imagine what you'll be doing 20 years from now?
B: I'll be in my 40s then. I'll probably be _____ my days _____ and gardening. Something _____ and boring, I _____.
A: Don't be so pessimistic. I'm hoping to retire earlier than anybody else in my office.
B: Oh, what _____ you _____ then?
A: I want to run marathons all over the world.
B: Marathons? You _____, _____ long running _____?
A: Exactly, full marathons. They have them everywhere now.
B: That's very _____. They say, "Youth is not a _____ of life; it's a _____ of mind." You can be living _____ of that.
A: Yes, I can and so can you. Why don't we try a marathon together?
B: What a great _____, Mark! You are so _____ and full of _____.
A: Yeah, think about what we can do after retirement, and really all through life.
B: Yes, I hadn't _____ about it like _____. You've just _____ my day. Thanks!

ACT OUT THE DIALOGUE

Work with your partner.
1. Silently and quickly read and remember one line at a time.
2. Look up at your partner and speak while keeping eye contact.
3. Change roles and practice again by replacing some parts with your own words.

111

Unit 11 Acupuncture — On Pins and Needles

QUESTIONS AND ANSWERS

Point to the acupuncture points on your body and discuss the affected areas with your partner.

1. What is this acupuncture point for?
2. Where is the point for treating (neck pain)?

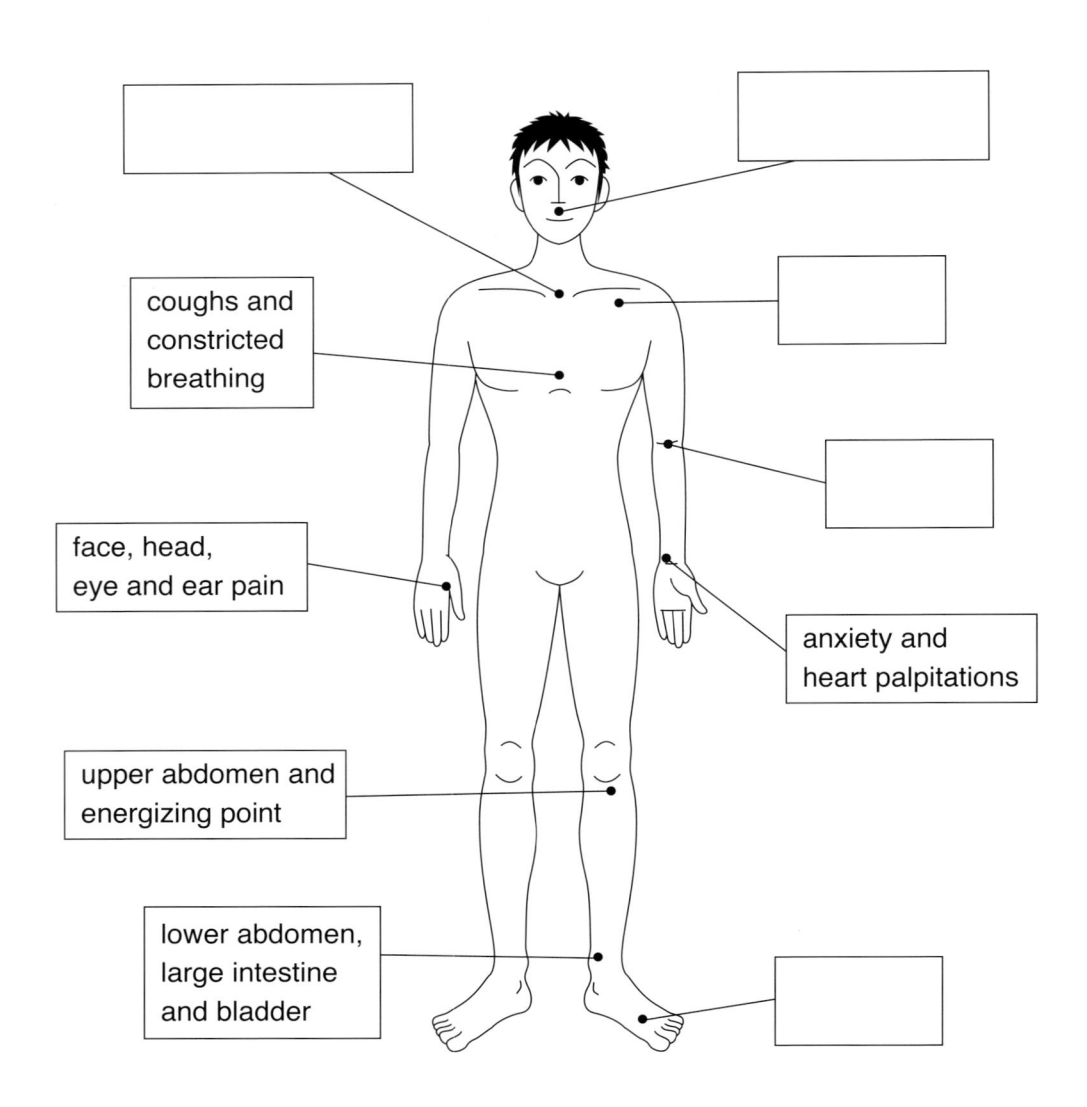

coughs and constricted breathing

face, head, eye and ear pain

upper abdomen and energizing point

lower abdomen, large intestine and bladder

anxiety and heart palpitations

Unit 11

Student B

MODEL DIALOGUE — JIGSAW LISTENING

Listen, repeat and fill in the blanks.

A: Hi, Ian. What are you doing to your arm with that pen?
B: Hi, Jackie. Can't _____ tell I'm _____ "shiatsu" therapy?
A: "Shiatsu"? What does that mean? Is that some kind of alternative medicine?
B: Yes, it's a kind of _____. Pressure is put on _____ points, usually with the _____, but sometimes with a _____ pen.
A: So, you mean, it's like acupuncture but uses fingers instead of needles?
B: Exactly. I'm _____ using my pen _____ of my _____.
A: Where's the point for a stiff neck? I always have aches in my neck and back, too.
B: Oh, you _____? Let me try my _____ pen on your shoulder. _____ on.
A: Well, actually, I'm already late and have to go. Thanks, anyway.
B: All right. Next time we _____, I'll show you some _____ points for _____ _____.
A: I'm sure I'll still have some sore spots then!

ACT OUT THE DIALOGUE

Work with your partner.
1. Silently and quickly read and remember one line at a time.
2. Look up at your partner and speak while keeping eye contact.
3. Change roles and practice again by replacing some parts with your own words.

Unit 12 Three Major Causes of Death — Are You Insured?

QUESTIONS AND ANSWERS

a. Memorize and ask these questions to Student A and complete your chart.
   1. Where is the (stomach) located?
   2. Could you draw the shape of the (stomach)?
   3. What is a function of the (stomach)?
   4. What is a possible illness of the (stomach)?

Name of Organ	Location	Shape	Function	Possible Illness
	tummy			ulcer
liver			to clean up blood	
	near the stomach			spleen cancer
intestines			to take in nutrition	
	in the abdominal cavity			kidney failure
pancreas			to make enzymes and insulin	

b. Answer the following questions.
   1. Which organ can work even if reduced to one quarter of its original size and is called "a silent organ"?
   2. Which organ is the appendix attached to?
   3. Which organ was believed to cause temper tantrums?

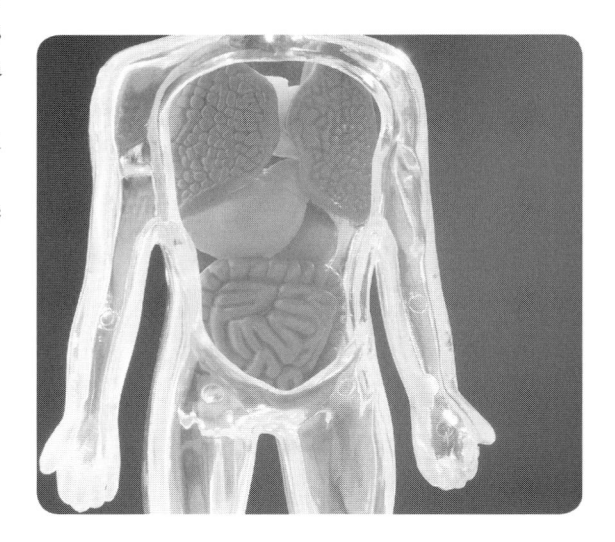

Unit 12

Student B

MODEL DIALOGUE — JIGSAW LISTENING

Listen, repeat and fill in the blanks.

A: Hi, Bill.
B: George, what's _____? You don't _____ _____ good.
A: I just had a squeezing pain in the center of my chest.
B: When _____ you have _____? How _____ did it _____?
A: Just now. I had chest pain and felt sick to my stomach. It seemed like forever.
B: Do you have _____ _____?
A: That was enough. I felt so bad in my chest, I didn't notice much else.
B: Did you feel like _____ or _____ out in _____ cold _____?
A: Yes, I did, actually. How did you know? My whole upper body felt funny, too.
B: Here, put this _____ under your _____. It _____ blood _____. You better have that _____ out right away.
A: Thank you. I'll go to the hospital right away. I'll go get my car.
B: Don't go _____ car. Let me _____ 9-1-1 for an _____.
A: Is it that serious?
B: It's _____ to be _____.

ACT OUT THE DIALOGUE

Work with your partner.
1. Silently and quickly read and remember one line at a time.
2. Look up at your partner and speak while keeping eye contact.
3. Change roles and practice again by replacing some parts with your own words.

Glossary

Unit 1
p. 7
- [ ] billion — [ ] 10億
- [ ] curiosity — [ ] 好奇心
- [ ] desire — [ ] 欲求
- [ ] detailed — [ ] 細かい
- [ ] diplomacy — [ ] 外交
- [ ] duty — [ ] 義務
- [ ] enable — [ ] 可能にする
- [ ] exact — [ ] 正確な
- [ ] galaxy — [ ] 銀河
- [ ] intelligent — [ ] 知的な
- [ ] knowledge — [ ] 知識
- [ ] lingua franca — [ ] 共通語
- [ ] morally — [ ] 道徳的に
- [ ] physician — [ ] 医師
- [ ] protect — [ ] 守る
- [ ] public — [ ] 公衆
- [ ] realize — [ ] 認識する
- [ ] remedy — [ ] 療法
- [ ] scholar — [ ] 学者
- [ ] specific — [ ] 特定な
- [ ] well-educated — [ ] 学のある

p. 8
- [ ] access — [ ] たどり着く
- [ ] analogy — [ ] 類推
- [ ] common — [ ] 一般的な
- [ ] curable — [ ] 治療可能な
- [ ] curious — [ ] 不思議な
- [ ] findings — [ ] 調査結果
- [ ] general — [ ] 一般的な
- [ ] journal article — [ ] 雑誌の記事
- [ ] papers — [ ] 論文
- [ ] particular — [ ] （ある）特定な
- [ ] rare — [ ] まれな
- [ ] require — [ ] 必要とする
- [ ] research — [ ] 研究
- [ ] responsibility — [ ] 責任
- [ ] shortage — [ ] 不足
- [ ] sight — [ ] 光景、視覚
- [ ] trapped — [ ] 捕らえられる
- [ ] unknown — [ ] 未知の
- [ ] virus — [ ] ウイルス

p. 9
- [ ] advanced — [ ] 進んだ
- [ ] chances — [ ] 確率
- [ ] decrease — [ ] 減少する
- [ ] duty — [ ] 義務
- [ ] Hangul — [ ] ハングル文字（語）
- [ ] remedy — [ ] 療法
- [ ] subjects — [ ] 課目
- [ ] tool — [ ] 道具
- [ ] universal — [ ] 普遍的な

p.10
- [ ] department — [ ] 部署、科
- [ ] dietitian — [ ] 栄養士
- [ ] first Language — [ ] 第1言語、母語
- [ ] gynecology — [ ] 婦人科
- [ ] occupation — [ ] 職業
- [ ] pregnant — [ ] 妊娠した
- [ ] psychiatry — [ ] 精神科
- [ ] surgery — [ ] 外科
- [ ] workplace — [ ] 職場

p.11
- [ ] limited — [ ] 制限された
- [ ] major — [ ] 主専攻
- [ ] medicine — [ ] 医学
- [ ] mind — [ ] 思考
- [ ] otherwise — [ ] そうでなければ
- [ ] replace — [ ] 置き換える
- [ ] role — [ ] 役割
- [ ] specialty — [ ] 専門
- [ ] well-rounded — [ ] 包括的な、円満な

p.12
- [ ] argument — [ ] 議論
- [ ] clinician — [ ] 臨床医（学者）

116

☐ competence	☐能力		☐ burn the midnight oil	☐徹夜する
☐ evaluate	☐評価する		☐ cheating	☐不正行為
☐ field	☐分野		☐ concentration	☐集中
☐ freshman	☐１年生		☐ consequence	☐結果
☐ senior	☐４年生		☐ essential	☐不可欠な
☐ sophomore	☐２年生		☐ fatigue	☐疲労
☐ statement	☐主張		☐ focus	☐集中する
☐ subsequently	☐結果的に		☐ gather	☐集める
☐ thesis	☐論文		☐ huge	☐巨大な
			☐ nap	☐仮眠

Unit 2
p.13

☐ accomplish	☐達成する		☐ recommend	☐推薦する
☐ achievement	☐達成		☐ refresh	☐気を新たにする
☐ arrogantly	☐横柄に		☐ sacrifice	☐犠牲
☐ associate	☐仲間		☐ stock up	☐たくわえる
☐ asthma	☐喘息		☐ survival	☐生存に関わる
☐ brag	☐自慢する		☐ torture	☐拷問
☐ chronic	☐慢性の		☐ temporary	☐一時的な
☐ colleague	☐同僚		☐ tiny	☐小さな

p.15

☐ continue	☐続く		☐ boss	☐上司
☐ deprivation	☐剥奪、欠乏		☐ jet lag	☐時差ボケ
☐ disorder	☐障害		☐ maintain	☐維持する
☐ drowsy	☐眠い		☐ oddly	☐奇妙にも
☐ dull	☐鈍い		☐ surplus	☐余分、余剰

p.17

☐ effort	☐努力		☐ insomnia	☐不眠
☐ exhaustion	☐疲労困憊		☐ pill	☐錠剤

p.18

☐ extreme	☐極端な		☐ hasty	☐早とちりな
☐ fatigue	☐疲労		☐ generalization	☐一般化的
☐ fellow	☐仲間			

Unit 3
p.19

☐ mental	☐精神的な		☐ allergy	☐アレルギー
☐ motivation	☐動機		☐ asbestos	☐アスベスト
☐ physical	☐身体的な		☐ calculate	☐計算する
☐ shortage	☐不足		☐ concern	☐懸念、関心
☐ surrender	☐放棄する		☐ estimate	☐見積もる
☐ typical	☐典型的な		☐ exposure	☐露出

p.14

☐ accomplishment	☐達成		☐ immune	☐免疫がある
☐ achieve	☐達成する		☐ intake	☐摂取
☐ acute	☐鋭い			
☐ awake	☐目覚めて			

117

☐ itch	☐ かゆみ		☐ unfamiliar	☐ なじみのない
☐ occur	☐ 起こる		**p.21**	
☐ poet	☐ 詩人		☐ current	☐ 現在の
☐ prevent	☐ 防ぐ		☐ diesel	☐ ディーゼル
☐ properly	☐ 適切に		☐ exhaust	☐ 排気
☐ scratch	☐ かすり傷		☐ experiment	☐ 実験
☐ shyness	☐ 恥じらい		☐ laboratory	☐ 実験室
☐ symptom	☐ 兆候		☐ nonexistent	☐ 実在しない、ない
☐ value	☐ 値		☐ prevention	☐ 防止
☐ unpleasant	☐ 不快な		☐ reaction	☐ 反応
p.20			☐ saline	☐ 塩水
☐ allergen	☐ アレルギー源		☐ scarce	☐ 不十分な
☐ cedar	☐ 杉		**p.22**	
☐ controlled	☐ 制御された		☐ eye drops	☐ 目薬
☐ disease	☐ 病気		☐ ointment	☐ 軟膏
☐ fit	☐ 発作		☐ crab	☐ カニ
☐ hay fever	☐ 花粉症		☐ shrimp	☐ エビ
☐ immune system	☐ 免疫システム		☐ ingredients	☐ 成分
☐ material	☐ 材料		☐ nausea	☐ 吐き気
☐ mountainous	☐ 山の多い		**p.23**	
☐ overact	☐ 大げさに演じる		☐ blow	☐ （鼻を）かむ
☐ overreact	☐ 過剰反応する		☐ dusty	☐ ほこりだらけの
☐ oversensitive	☐ 神経過敏な		☐ scratchy	☐ ちくちくする
☐ oversimplify	☐ 単純化しすぎる		☐ stuffy	☐ （鼻が）詰まった
☐ pollen	☐ 花粉		☐ throat	☐ のど
☐ pollution	☐ 汚染		**p.24**	
☐ react	☐ 反応する		☐ bacteria	☐ バクテリア
☐ rub	☐ こする、なでる		☐ bathtub	☐ 浴槽
☐ runny	☐ どろっとした		☐ cilia	☐ 繊毛
☐ sensitive	☐ 敏感な		☐ confuse	☐ 混乱させる
☐ sneezing	☐ くしゃみ		☐ consequence	☐ 結果
☐ stuffy	☐ 詰まった、息苦しい		☐ continuously	☐ 絶え間なく
☐ sufferer	☐ 苦しんでいる人		☐ cypress bath	☐ ひのき風呂
☐ substance	☐ 物質		☐ germ	☐ 細菌
☐ symptomatic	☐ 症状の		☐ membrane	☐ 膜
☐ treatment	☐ 治療、処理		☐ sequence	☐ 時間の流れ
☐ uncontrolled	☐ 非制御の		☐ stomach	☐ 胃

■ Unit 4 以降の glossary は下記のサイトからダウンロードしてください。
　http://www.kinsei-do.co.jp/4010/4010_glossary.pdf

本書にはCD（別売）があります

Health Matters
英語で知る健康問題

2009年2月1日 初版第1刷発行
2024年4月10日 改訂新版第10刷発行

著者 　藤 井 哲 郎
　　　　Adam Murray

発行者 　福 岡 正 人
発行所 　株式会社 金 星 堂
（〒101-0051）東京都千代田区神田神保町 3-21
　　　　　　Tel.(03) 3263-3828（営業部）
　　　　　　　(03) 3263-3997（編集部）
　　　　　　Fax (03) 3263-0716
　　　　　　https://www.kinsei-do.co.jp

印刷所・製本所／興亜産業　　　Printed in Japan
本書の無断複製・複写は著作権法上での例外を除き禁じられています。本書を代行業者等の第三者に依頼してスキャンやデジタル化することは、たとえ個人や家庭内での利用であっても認められておりません。
落丁・乱丁本はお取り替えいたします。
ISBN978-4-7647-4010-5　C1082

Student CD Track List

Track	Activity	Track	Activity
1	Title		**Assignment Dictation**
	Model Dialogue	14	Unit 1
2	Unit 1	15	Unit 2
3	Unit 2	16	Unit 3
4	Unit 3	17	Unit 4
5	Unit 4	18	Unit 5
6	Unit 5	19	Unit 6
7	Unit 6	20	Unit 7
8	Unit 7	21	Unit 8
9	Unit 8	22	Unit 9
10	Unit 9	23	Unit 10
11	Unit 10	24	Unit 11
12	Unit 11	25	Unit 12
13	Unit 12		

To the Students
How to Use the Student CD and Assignment Task Sheets

The Student CD includes ASSIGNMENT DICTATION: four statements and one personal question for each unit. The statements and the question are read twice. The first time is at natural speed for listening practice and the second time is at a reduced speed for listen and repeat practice – shadowing. Write every word of the four sentences and write your own answer to the personal question – e.g. If the CD asks "Where are you from?," write the name of your hometown.

The Student CD also includes MODEL DIALOGUE for you to practice conversations without a conversation partner. The audio for speaker A is recorded in one channel and the audio for speaker B is recorded in the other channel. For example, if you want to practice the lines for speaker B, listen to only the recording of speaker A by using only one earphone and speaking at the appropriate times. Of course, by listening with the other earphone, the lines for speaker A can be practiced.

Unit 1 Task Sheet

name:　　　　　　　　　no:　　　date:　 /　 /　　score:　5

1.
2.
3.
4.
5. Your answer

---- キリトリ線 ----

Unit 2 Task Sheet

name:　　　　　　　　　no:　　　date:　 /　 /　　score:　5

1.
2.
3.
4.
5. Your answer

---- キリトリ線 ----

Unit 3 Task Sheet

name:　　　　　　　　　no:　　　date:　 /　 /　　score:　5

1.
2.
3.
4.
5. Your answer

Unit 4 Task Sheet

name: no: date: / /   score:

1.
2.
3.
4.
5. Your answer

---- キリトリ線 ----

Unit 5 Task Sheet

name: no: date: / /   score:

1.
2.
3.
4.
5. Your answer

---- キリトリ線 ----

Unit 6 Task Sheet

name: no: date: / /   score:

1.
2.
3.
4.
5. Your answer

Unit 7
Task Sheet

name:　　　　　　　　　no:　　　date:　/　/　　score:

1.
2.
3.
4.
5. Your answer

---- キリトリ線 ----

Unit 8
Task Sheet

name:　　　　　　　　　no:　　　date:　/　/　　score:

1.
2.
3.
4.
5. Your answer

---- キリトリ線 ----

Unit 9
Task Sheet

name:　　　　　　　　　no:　　　date:　/　/　　score:

1.
2.
3.
4.
5. Your answer

Unit 10 Task Sheet

name: no: date: / / score:

1.
2.
3.
4.
5. Your answer

---- キリトリ線 ----

Unit 11 Task Sheet

name: no: date: / / score:

1.
2.
3.
4.
5. Your answer

---- キリトリ線 ----

Unit 12 Task Sheet

name: no: date: / / score:

1.
2.
3.
4.
5. Your answer

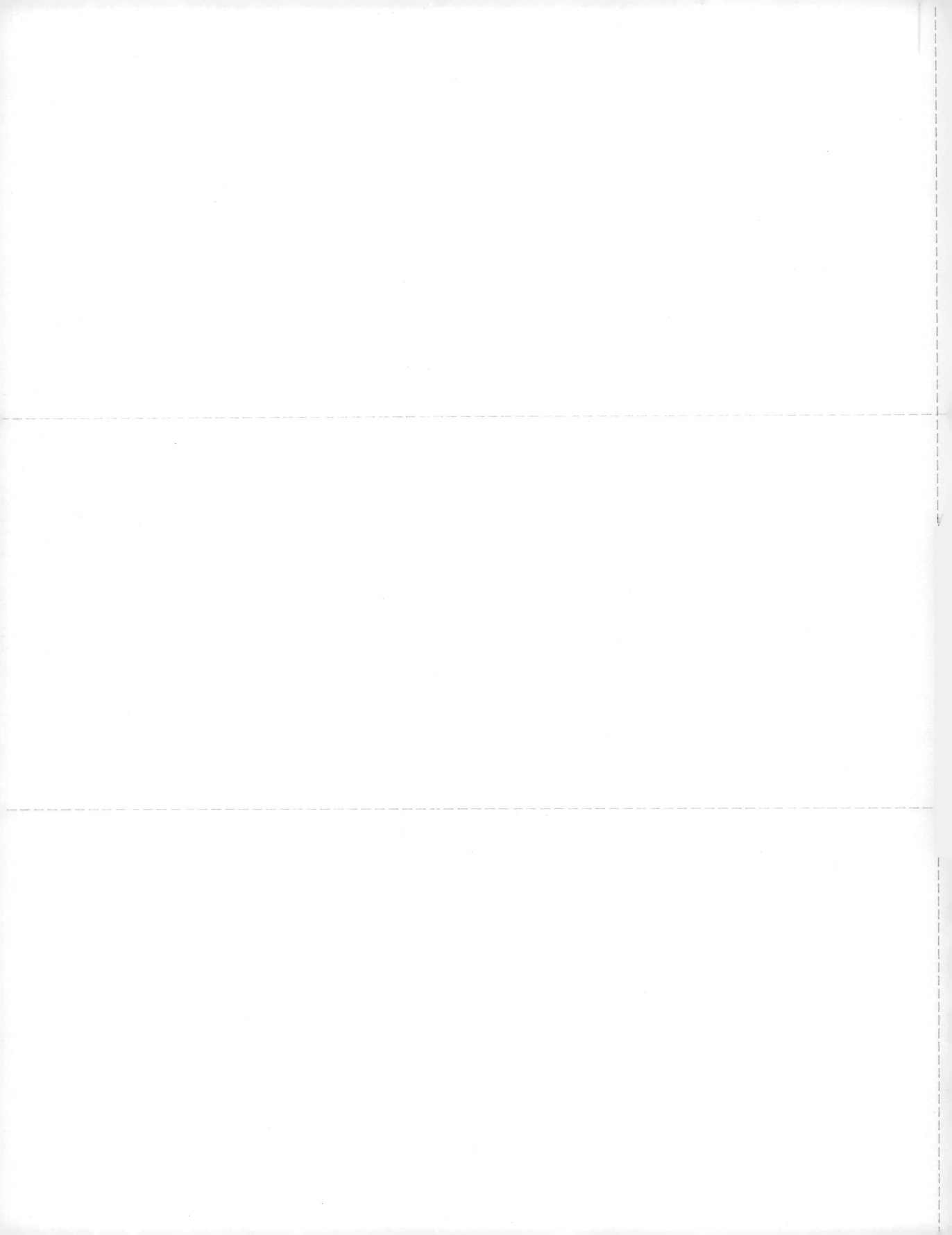